Mrs Cowan's Boy

Mrs Cowan's Boy

RORY COWAN

Gill Books

Gill Books
Hume Avenue
Park West
Dublin 12
www.gillbooks.ie

Gill Books is an imprint of M.H. Gill and Co.

978 07171 8341 8

Edited by Alison Walsh
Design and print origination by O'K Graphic Design, Dublin
Proofread by Djinn von Noorden
Printed by CPI Group (UK) Ltd, Croydon CRO 4YY
This book is typeset in 11/16 pt Sabon MT.

The paper used in this book comes from the wood pulp of managed forests. For every tree felled, at least one tree is planted, thereby renewing natural resources.

A CIP catalogue record for this book is available from the British Library.

5 4 3 2 1

*To my mother, Esther Cowan, who I'm really
proud to have called 'Ma'.*

CONTENTS

PROLOGUE

Young at Heart

One of my favourite photographs is of my mother and father and me on the beach in Rush. It was the summer of 1968 and I was nine years old, so my parents were only in their mid-thirties and yet they look much older in the photo. Da is wearing his summer outfit: his best socks and sandals, teamed with navy shorts and a shirt. Ma is in one of her homemade summer dresses, her hands placed on my shoulders. She has a fixed smile on her face and I'm prepared to bet that it was because I'd just been in trouble for doing something silly. I wasn't a bold child, but trouble used to find me and one of Ma's refrains was that she'd send me to Artane Industrial School. Parenting was different then!

As I write this, it's 15 July 2019, my sixtieth birthday – almost twice as old as they were in the photograph. Both

Ma and Da are gone, and I realise that it's up to me now. I'm the adult. I can't help wondering how on earth that happened. Where did the time go? The changes are physical and mental, good and bad. Physically, it's no picnic. In my head, I'm still in my twenties, but when I get up in the morning and lurch sleepily to the bathroom, have a pee and then look in the mirror, my granddad looks back at me. And my reaction is the same every time. My scream sends the cats running down the stairs, letting out yowls to tell me they want to get out of the house as fast as possible. How did it happen that I went to bed as an energetic young man and over the next eight hours turned into *Corrie*'s favourite old dame, Vera Duckworth?

I lower my head and look at the rest of my body. Where did those moobs come from? In Australia, a beer belly is known affectionately as 'the verandah over the toy shop'. When I was my thirties, I started to get a verandah of my own. Somebody looked at my beer belly once and said, 'What beer are you drinking to give you a belly like that?'

I replied, 'There's a tap underneath it, if you want a taste.'

It's hard to believe that it all happened so fast. While I used to scoff at comments my parents made when I was young, and pooh-poohed their clichés, they were right about one thing (well, they were right about nearly everything, as it turns out), when they said, 'time goes by so fast'. During the last few years I've seen my doctor more often than I've seen my friends. There are aches and pains I never had when I was younger and now the only groaning noises I make in bed are because of my bad back. I'm sure my doctor has put all his children through university on the money I've paid him over the last ten years. He's inviting me to his son's college graduation and during his speech, I expect the boy to thank me for making it all happen for him. But I'm not bitching and moaning. Well maybe I am, just a little bit.

I know that ageing is very different nowadays. Back then, you were old when you hit 40, probably due to a combination of poor diet and smoking, not to mention having children younger. My da was only 43 when he had a heart attack, can you imagine? Now, thankfully, I'm fitter than I've ever been. Exercise and eating well helps, but so does a bit of Botox and fillers – yes, I'm not above a little chemical help now and again! However, like my father, I am losing my hair. He lost his getting older, while I'm losing mine because of years bleaching it. And a balding scalp is ageing. I asked my doctor about it, hoping he could give me a course of tablets or creams to make my hair grow back, but there was nothing he could give me. He did advise that I could get a transplant, but I thought I'd look ridiculous with a kidney on my head.

There are many other things I notice about getting older. The change in libido for one thing. When you're young, your libido drags you along as it rushes through your every waking moment. At sixty, it starts to crawl. When I was in my twenties and thirties, myself and my friends would enjoy looking at all the handsome young men in the bars. Now, we talk about what nice restaurants we've been to and how that popular gay destination, Sitges, is not what it used to be. We don't even see the gorgeous young men anymore, because that would mean putting on our glasses when we're out in public. And, to many gay men, that's a bridge too far. These days, when I think of 'hooking up', it's more likely to be to a machine that does liver scans or blood pressure.

Another thing about getting older is an increasing need for colonoscopies. Once you hit fifty, they become part of your year. The whole procedure is horrible. I won't describe it in this book, but if you want to know what one is, then Google is your friend. When I went in to have my first one about ten years ago, I thought the situation needed to be lightened. The doctor, a middle-aged man, told me what they would be doing after the anaesthetic had taken effect and I was asleep. To cover my embarrassment, I coyly said, 'Are you really a doctor? Because, if you're not, I think that you should buy me a drink before you get familiar with that part of my body.' Needless to say, that comment went down like a fart in a spacesuit, as Billy Connolly put it. And did I learn to keep my mouth shut? Of course I didn't. The next year, when I was wheeled into the operating theatre to have colonoscopy number two, I announced cheerily, 'If you find a hat box and a pair of slingbacks up there, I know who owns them.' The doctor looked at me as if he was looking at a skid-mark on a hotel towel in Ballybunion.

I can see the funny side, though, and one of my favourite jokes deals with colonoscopies. Two old dears, Gladys and Sadie, are waiting in the doctor's surgery and get talking. Gladys says, 'What are you in for, love?'

Sadie replies, 'I'm having a camera put down my throat.'

And Gladys pipes up, 'You'd better go in first, love, because I'm having it shoved up my arse.' If you didn't laugh, you'd cry.

Mentally, my parents had a really positive attitude to life and I plan to copy that. In my youth, I thought that they didn't have a clue – who does? – but now I appreciate the wisdom that came with them getting older, and their energy. When Da hit sixty-five, and was entitled to free travel on buses and trains, he'd get up in the morning and say to my mother, 'Esther, do you fancy going out for lunch today?' And if she said yes, which she always did, he'd say, 'Well, get yourself ready and we'll get the bus to Heuston Station and the train to Galway.' And off they'd go to have lunch in Galway, or Limerick, or Cork – whichever train was leaving first. The idea of sitting in the house, like it was God's waiting room, waiting to be called home, was not something they relished. They'd get up and get out and do something. As an adult, I could never just pop in to see them during the day; I'd have to make an appointment. And that's because they were never home. They'd be off visiting some museum or art gallery in some part of the country.

That attitude of 'when you stop, you die' is how I plan on living the rest of my life, even if my mind says I'm in my twenties and my body says, 'Yeah, you wish.' As you'll see in the book, I gave my body a fair old bashing, but unlike my Da, I was lucky enough to have benefited from the great improvements in healthcare of the last twenty years or so.

I want to use my time wisely, just like they did. I wish that Ma hadn't developed dementia in her later years, as it was sad to see her decline, but she never lost her spirit, or her sense of humour. Nor did she lose that habit of speaking her mind! I think I take after her in that respect.

Joking aside, it doesn't seem that long ago that I was a small child living in a small two-up two-down in Kylemore Drive, Ballyfermot. It's nearly sixty years since we moved there and fifty since we left, but I can still see myself, as if in an old film reel, singing along to Sandie Shaw's hit single and Eurovision winner 'Puppet on a String', which played on our Dansette record player in the kitchen back in 1967. It's a house filled with memories. That house was an essential part of my childhood. Dublin Corporation might have built it, but it played a big part in building me. In that little house, I learned all the important lessons in life, from good manners to self-discipline, to having the time for a laugh and a bit of fun. I learned to love music, a passion that's been part of my life ever since; I learned the importance of community spirit and of people looking out for each other. Life can be tough, as we all know, but those years in Ballyfermot gave me a grounding in how to deal with life's ups and downs.

My mother Esther ruled that house, like so many women at the time, but it was she who encouraged me always to be myself. Being gay was something we never discussed openly – like so many things at that time – but there's no way I could have been as happy as I was to be a gay man in Dublin in the seventies and eighties if my mother hadn't told me never to follow the crowd, not to be afraid to stand out, and to be me. Whenever I came home wearing the fashion of the day, she'd say, 'Oh, yes, go ahead and be a sheep!' With my mother in charge, there was never any danger of that. To her, standing out was more important than fitting in. She always said, 'Be good or be bad, but never be average. If you're good or bad at something, that means that at least you tried.' I can still remember her giving out to one of my teachers who told her that I was an 'average' student. 'My son is *not* average,' my mother told him firmly. She might have given me 'notions', but she also gave me self-confidence.

I credit both my mother and father with giving me the courage to try new things, whether it was a job as a stock controller at EMI – thanks to a holiday job in a record shop that my dad got me – or going on stage in *Mrs Brown's Boys*, with a day's notice, in 2000. Whenever I was presented with an opportunity, I'd think 'I can do that,' and that's thanks to my father, but particularly to my mother. In so many respects, I really am my mother's son, Mrs Cowan's Boy.

ONE

Kooks

It's a funny thing, but it's only when you get the opportunity to write about your life that you start to think about who you are and where you came from. When I was young, my mother used to tell me lots of stories about growing up in Rathfarnham, at the foot of the Dublin Mountains, but I can't say I took much notice of them. How I wish I'd listened more! Now my parents are both gone, Da in 2008 and Ma in 2018 after a long battle with dementia, and I'll never be able to ask them about their formative years. It's the same for everyone, I suppose. We think our parents arrived just as they are, middle-aged, worrying about the mortgage, we forget that they were young once, just like us, and that they had their own stories, their own lives before we came along and ruined them.

I often wondered why my mother never talked much about marrying my father, but I was later to find out that there was a reason. Ma and Da met in November 1955. Da's mother, my grandmother, had just died of cancer and my father's friends had brought him to a ceilí in the Mansion House to cheer him up. And there my mother was. I know that they got married in 1958, somewhere in London, but it was always shrouded in mystery. I learned that Da had gone to England to work as a bus driver, and Ma had followed him soon after, to work at the sweet counter in a Woolworth's store. That was all they'd tell me – and the reason for the secrecy was that they were living together, 'in sin', which was quite a big deal in the 1950s. I found this out because I asked Ma one day why she was always cool towards Da's sister Deirdre and why herself and Deirdre weren't close.

Apparently, back in 1958 there had been a party, probably in some Irish area of London, and a load of my father's eleven brothers and sisters had turned up. Ma said, 'I remember that somebody asked me where I lived, and I told them: "We have a flat around the corner." Then Deirdre pipes up, "It's one room!", shouting across the crowd!' Ma was mortified, because she thought that she was being put down for living in a bedsit and not in a flat or a house, but in telling me the story, my mother had unwittingly let the cat out of the bag: she and Dad had been living together. At that time living together before you were married, particularly if you were Irish, was something you kept to yourself. From that moment on, my mother had a frosty relationship with

Deirdre. Esther knew how to hold a grudge – a regular saying of hers was, 'You only get one chance to insult me.' Nobody ever got a second chance! The irony of Ma's choice to live with Dad wasn't lost on me: years later, when I rented my first proper apartment, sharing it with my great friend Annette Carroll, my mother nearly had a heart attack. 'Living in sin' she called it. If she only knew! She didn't want me to do my own thing, even though she'd done hers.

I do know that my mother and father came from totally different classes: my mother from a labourer's cottage in Rathfarnham, my father from a grand house in Clontarf, complete with grounds and staff. I also know that my mother was born when her mother was fifty – can you imagine? I can still see the chickens Granny kept in the back garden in Willbrook, beside the Tuning Fork pub, even though by the time I was a child of three or four, Granny was dying. In fact, hers was the first dead body I ever saw.

When Brigid Doyle died on 28 September 1963, my younger brother Gerard and I were brought over to the house to see her. I had no idea that she was actually dead until I was taken into her bedroom and there she was, laid out in the bed. I thought she was asleep. My mother had to explain that the sleep was permanent. Ma's father, Patrick Doyle from Clanbrassil Street, had died in 1943, when she was ten. He was a garden labourer, along with one of his brothers, Tommy. A wealthy family called the Careys had a huge farm up the road in Rathfarnham, so Granddad worked there, cutting the growth back, pruning, mowing. My mother always said that they could look at a tree and tell you how old it was. There was nothing they didn't know about nature.

As you can imagine, my mother's family were poor, and in those days, long before social welfare benefits, poor really did mean poor. When I bought my first home, Ma would come down and open the fridge and look in. If there was nothing there, she'd ask me if I needed a loan! If the fridge was full, she'd exclaim, 'Now, that's a good fridge.' To my mother, food was wealth. An empty larder was not a good thing. Food was the number-one priority for my mother's family, and I still laugh when I recall the nicknames Auntie Mag, my mother's sister, had for Gerard and me. My brother was 'my old ham bone', and I was 'rasher'.

Born in April 1933, Ma – Esther – was the youngest of seven children. Her mother had had fourteen pregnancies in all, and seven miscarriages. Of the seven children who had lived, two, Brigid and Patrick, died before they were ten. So there were five left: Peter, Tom, Mag, Eileen and Esther, the youngest, all crammed into a tiny worker's cottage in Rathfarnham.

Eileen was Ma's next-oldest sister, but she was five years older, so I don't think Ma was expected at all. You know how it is with youngest children – they get what they want, they get their way, and Ma was always strong-willed. She and Eileen were very close. Every Wednesday night, Eileen would come to visit, and every Saturday we'd take the bus from Ballyfermot to Rathfarnham to visit her.

But the real character in Ma's family was my mother's eldest sister. Margaret, or Mag as she was known, was a big woman with a great sense of humour, and she loved a good sing-song. She was also a fierce republican and a lifelong member of Cumann na mBan. Because of that, she came to the notice of the gardaí back in the 1940s and stayed on their radar for decades afterwards. I remember her hanging black flags out of her window when the hunger strikers died in the Maze Prison in 1981, and she would stick posters of Margaret Thatcher in her window with the tagline 'Wanted for Murder'. I know she was interned in Mountjoy Prison in the early 1940s and she was held there for two years, after being questioned in relation to the murder of a policeman, Dinny O'Brien. My mother told me that she and my granny used to visit her there as often as they could.

In 1951 Mag married a man called Fritz Langsdorf, who'd come from Germany to Ireland in the 1930s and immediately joined the IRA. He was known as the 'German IRA man' – so much for a secret organisation. My assistant, Avri Citron, and I did a bit of digging in the National Library and found that Langsdorf served many sentences for republican activities. According to material that Avri and I found, he was interned in Arbour Hill, the Curragh and Mountjoy at various times between 1934 and 1945.

I was well aware that my mother came from a republican family, and even though – unlike Mag – she wasn't active, I can recall her telling me that she used to sell Easter lily badges outside the church to commemorate the Rising. Being so young, only six or seven, she used to sell hundreds of them. One day, a garda tried to confiscate all her badges and my mother told me that a bus driver, a huge big man who'd seen the commotion, stopped his bus, jumped off, leaving his bewildered passengers wondering why a bus had stopped in the middle of the road, and threatened the garda: 'You lay one finger on her and I'll tear the head off you. Her family has been selling lilies outside this church for years.' The garda slunk off with his tail between his legs.

Their grandfather was Peter Doyle, one of the famous Invincibles – the hit squad, for want of a better word, which had split off from the IRB and which was involved in the Phoenix Park murders. Peter was questioned, but not charged – but I can see where Mag's republicanism came from.

However, it was her escapades with the law towards the end of her life that still tickle me. She always loved a good protest, and in the eighties she decided she wasn't going to pay her TV licence because of RTÉ's controversial Section 31, under which the voices of Sinn Féin members on TV were dubbed over by actors.

She explained her decision to the TV licence inspector, and a few weeks later, she received a summons and had to go to court. She explained why she was refusing to pay her TV licence and was promptly sentenced to one day in jail. For whatever reason, she had to serve her sentence in Limerick Prison. So she was driven in a garda car, with two gardaí escorting her, the 125 miles to Limerick. She was delivered to the prison and the two gardaí left and drove back to Dublin. By the time Mag was processed and given her tea, her day's sentence was complete. Two more gardaí from the local station in Limerick were tasked with driving her back home to Dublin. Mag loved the fact that she had caused the state and the gardaí so much trouble and expense.

However, a few months later she was back in court again. This time she thought it best to give a different reason for not having a TV licence, so when she was asked by the judge to explain herself, she said, 'I'm not paying for a TV licence because there are not enough programmes in Irish on RTÉ.'

'Ah, I see,' said the judge. 'Well, if you're that much in favour of the Irish language, I suggest we conduct the rest of this case in Irish.' It turned out that the judge was a fluent Irish speaker and Mag couldn't speak it at all. She was sentenced to two days in Mountjoy Prison and she served the full two days.

When my mother was thirteen or fourteen, she got TB – tuberculosis. One of her sisters had brought her a brooch that was green and Granny had said, 'Throw that away. Green is for grief.' Two weeks later, my mother was diagnosed with TB. Granny said, 'See? That's that brooch.' That's the power of superstition: you put a brooch on and you get TB! Ma was convinced that it was all because of the green brooch, and when I said, 'Ma, you'd have got TB anyway,' she wouldn't listen. Loads of her friends died of TB and apparently at the time she was a child up to 10,000 people a year died of TB in Dublin, more than half of them children.

I once bought a lovely suit – this was in the eighties, and the shirt was longer than the jacket, which had tails. And the trousers were stripy. Boy George was all the rage then and I was delighted with myself; I thought I was dressing just like him. The suit cost me something like £360 – it was an imported Italian suit – and when I went out in it, it was as if I'd arrived. Eventually I stopped wearing it, figuring that it wasn't really me, but then one day I went to look for it, thinking I might give it another airing. I was still living at home at the time and I said to Ma, 'Where's that suit gone?'

'Oh, I threw it in the bin,' she told me. She'd taken this very expensive suit out of the wardrobe and thrown it in the bin! 'The suit's green,' she explained, 'and green is for grief.'

I could hardly blame her for being so superstitious because after her diagnosis, my mother spent the next two years in bed. The doctors wanted to send her away to a sanatorium outside the city to recover, but Granny wouldn't let her go. Instead, she took Ma out of hospital and home to bed and all her friends had to talk to her through her bedroom window. Granny took a big risk nursing my mother at home, because TB was very infectious. In fact, I came across a poster from that time that said, 'Don't Spit: Spitting Spreads Disease'.

And if TB didn't kill you, something else would. My uncle Harry, who was married to my auntie Eileen, died of kidney disease in 1964, aged just thirty-seven. He and Eileen were my godparents and he used to come to Ballyfermot on a Friday and take me over to their home in Churchtown to stay the night. I remember going to visit him in the old Skin and Cancer Hospital, as it was then known – 'for the treatment of diseases of the skin, cancer, rodent ulcer, lupus, kidney and other urinary diseases' – on Hume Street.

I was not yet five years old, but I remember the day he died, 1 March. Eileen had taken me to Mass in her local church. During Mass, my mother ran down to the shop to get magazines and fruit to bring in to Harry in hospital later that day, and the next thing, a man walked into the church and strode up to the altar, muttering something into the priest's ear. The image is still clear in my mind, because at the time it was a mortal sin to go past the altar rails and I expected a bolt of lightning to strike the man down. Then the priest asked if Mrs Eileen Gibson would go to the front door of the church. I can still see her in her Sunday best, walking all by herself to the door, where the gardaí were waiting. I was frightened, so I tried to catch up with her, standing beside her while the gardaí told her that her husband had died, whereupon she collapsed on the floor.

Eventually the gardaí got her home and one of them gave me sixpence. 'Look after your auntie,' he said. I nodded solemnly, all of four-and-a-half years old. The next few days would be spent watching Ma making sandwiches and Eileen howling. I tried to get her to stop, but she couldn't. Harry was so young, and so was Eileen.

After Harry died, Eileen became a bigger part of our lives. Eileen and Harry had had no children and my mother didn't want her sister left at home on her own, so it became the norm that Eileen would visit us after work on Wednesday evening and we would go and spend all day Saturday in her house with her. If my mother was bringing us to the cinema,

Eileen would come with us, as she would on outings and holidays. For our First Communions and school plays, Eileen was always there. She joined us for Christmas every year, too, arriving on Christmas Eve and staying until just after New Year. We loved Eileen and we were all delighted when, in the mid-seventies, she got married again to a man she worked with, Andy O'Neill. Andy was fantastic and they were very happy together for years until his death.

My father's upbringing was similar to my mother's, in that he was brought up a Catholic and a socialist, and, indeed, a republican, but in other ways they couldn't have been more different. Born on 30 April 1931, Rory senior was one of eleven children. He grew up in a grand house on the Malahide Road and, unlike my mother, never had to worry about there being food on the table. He had a keen social awareness, which came from his father, Captain Peadar Cowan, a Labour Party member, who later joined Clann na Poblachta and became a TD in 1948, then represented Dublin North-East as an independent. He was well known for having supported Noël Browne and his Mother and Child Scheme against the Church, and you can imagine how that went down.

When I was a child at school, the priest would come in to the classroom and he'd say, 'Rory Cowan ... are you any relation to Peadar Cowan?'

'Yes, he's my granddad,' I'd reply. When I'd go home later, I'd tell Ma and Da all about the priest asking questions, and Da would ask, 'What did you say?'

'I told him that my granddad was Peadar Cowan,' I'd say, and then Ma and Da would both laugh. I never knew why until much later. Recently, Avri and I looked him up and discovered things about him that my father never told me and that suddenly make a lot of sense.

I have only one memory of Da's father. We visited him in a council house in Killester, which I now know to be the place where he moved after his time in jail. In 1955 his wife, Rosemary, died and his world fell apart over the next seven years. I can still remember Da carrying me in and introducing me to this old man in a big army coat, which he was probably wearing because the place was so cold. He was only fifty-eight, younger than I am now, but to me he seemed ancient. I can't remember how long the visit lasted, but eventually Da said, 'Say goodbye to your granddad,' and I waved. I never saw him again.

I know that my grandfather was an original thinker, and that he seems to have been the kind of person who stuck to his principles no matter what. After falling out with the Labour Party, because he set up a rogue republican group called Vanguard, he became the treasurer of Clann na Poblachta, until he fell out with them, again on a matter of principle. Some party members went to a conference in Rome and Peadar insisted that German people had to be punished for their part in World War II. They were not to be forgiven, Peadar felt, but the rest of the party disagreed with him. Peadar became an independent TD at the general election of 1948 and that probably suited him – he just wasn't the kind of man to give up on his principles for the sake of toeing the party line.

He did two things that made me very proud. After leaving the Irish Army, he trained as a solicitor. After World War II, thousands of Irish men returned from fighting as part of the British Army. Among them were 5,700 so-called deserters, who'd left the Irish Army to fight in the British ranks. Some of the soldiers had only been released from German POW camps just before their return, to find the Military Police waiting for them on the docks as they disembarked from the ships that had taken them home. Two of them, privates Patrick Shannon and Patrick Kehoe, were to be court-martialled in June 1945, and Peadar was representing them.

It was a show trial, intended to make examples of these men who'd fought with the British. Peadar made the case that they couldn't be deserters, because the definition of deserter implied that a soldier had left a place of danger to go to a place of safety; but these two had done the exact opposite, and had fought in North Africa, Sicily and mainland Italy. So they couldn't be deserters. Patrick Shannon had left the Irish Army because he couldn't support his mother on his low wages. Peadar also claimed that in any other country in the world, these two men would be welcomed home as heroes. However, anti-British feelings were high in Ireland at the time and Peadar, this former republican, was never really going to win the case. The two privates were formally dismissed, stripped of pay and pension rights and deprived of the right to claim unemployment benefits.

I next came across Peadar in transcripts that we found from Dáil Éireann, which mention that he'd taken up the case of a boy in Artane Industrial School who'd been beaten by a young religious brother, so badly that his arm was broken. The youngster's mother hadn't been allowed to see him, so she'd come to see Peadar, then a TD. Peadar raised the matter in the Dáil, which wasn't popular. The then Minister for Education described it as an 'isolated incident'. Knowing what we now know, I wonder if he was right. Peadar had partial success in that a rule was introduced that corporal punishment could only be doled out in industrial schools by people with experience. Young brothers were no longer allowed to do it. It would seem that you had to beat the children in the right way!

What I find very sad is that Peadar died with just £5 to his name and having served a year in jail for embezzlement. It seems that after his wife died he just couldn't cope. He was struck off the register and didn't practise again, dying in poverty in 1962.

My father was a republican, like his father. Even though he'd gone to the UK to find work, like so many other people at the time, when Ma was pregnant with me, Da sent her home because he didn't want a child of his born in the UK. Ma had seen so much growing up – her sister and brother-in-law interned and her house constantly being raided – that she didn't want it for her family, so there really wasn't any republican influence on me. I remember that old friends from the Labour Party, like John O'Connell and David Thornley, would drop by and I'd listen to them discuss politics; old

IRA members, like Rory Brady, or Ruairí Ó Brádaigh, as he was also known, would come to the house and I'd be introduced and told to go out and play. It was never pushed on me or discussed. We would go to Bodenstown, but it was just a day out for me and, while Da went on republican marches, he never asked me to go. He was always protesting about something, though. He was very much against the Iraq War, I recall. I wasn't – I couldn't understand why he was marching to keep a gay-hating despot in power!

As you can imagine, Da was not a fan of the Catholic Church. He never brought us to Mass – only to our First Holy Communions. When we were still living in Ballyfermot – we moved to Athlone when I was ten, then Limerick for a couple of years – my mother would drag us out to Mass, and if there were sodalities or novenas, she would be as close to the altar rails as anyone could get. The local priest would wonder why Da wasn't there and questions would be asked – was Ma, with her three kids, a widow? One priest came to visit and when he sat down in the living room he started asking questions about Da.

'What does your husband do?'

'He works for the ITGWU – the Irish Transport and General Workers' Union,' Ma explained.

'Oh, is he a communist?' the priest asked.

'No, he's a trade unionist,' Ma retorted. She was religious, but she was also fiercely protective of her family and she'd defend them against any accusations.

Then the priest caught sight of the George Bernard Shaw Toby jug, which took pride of place on top of the china cabinet. (In case you're wondering, Toby jugs were very popular in my mother's day. I wonder whether jugs in the shape of famous people's faces would be quite the thing today.)

'Is that Lenin?' he asked.

'No, Father,' Ma said. 'If you knew anything about literature, you'd know it was George Bernard Shaw.' Even though my mother had left school at thirteen, she was incredibly well read and was familiar with *Pygmalion*, *Caesar and Cleopatra* and with Shaw's other works. 'You should read him, father. He's a lot to say about the clergy!'

Da continued his own father's legacy, taking up the cause of battered wives, as they were known then, and of the Travelling community. He'd often bring me to the halting site near Ballyfermot and he'd insist we always referred to Travellers as exactly that – Travellers, not any of the nasty names they were often called. Coincidentally, his work brought him in touch with Brendan O'Carroll's mother, Maureen, who was a very well-known Labour Party TD, when he was trying to find shelter for women who'd had to leave home in a hurry. He'd ring her and he'd say, 'Maureen, I have a woman, four kids and nowhere to go.'

'Rory, we're full up,' Maureen would say, but when Da explained the situation, she never refused to take someone in. However, as far as Da was concerned the Catholic Church was simply a money-making machine. He'd worked in Dublin Corporation, as it was known then, before the ITGWU, and he'd seen how the Church would take kids from their families and place them in children's homes. Da would often go to court to see what was happening with a family who'd approached him, and he'd see a priest there looking to take the children and put them to work in places like Letterfrack and Artane industrial schools. They'd say, 'That woman can't look after kids on her own, without her husband.' At that time, everything financial was in the husband's name, so if a couple broke up the woman had to leave the home, if it was rented, and she wasn't entitled to anything. So the argument was that she couldn't look after the kids. The Church was complicit in forcing families apart, which is why Da hated the Catholic Church as an institution.

My parents' principles were born from their heritage and life experiences and they stuck with those principles throughout their lives.

TWO

☆

Always Something
There to Remind
Me

Number 61 Kylemore Drive was my home until the age of ten and I think that it shaped me more than anywhere else I've ever lived. It was an ordinary council home: it had two rooms downstairs and two bedrooms and a bathroom upstairs, with a good-sized front and back garden. Downstairs consisted of the kitchen, which we basically lived in when we weren't in bed, and the front room, or parlour as it was called, which, as children, we weren't allowed into on pain of death – it was strictly for visitors. The parlour had a carpet, a two-seater sofa, a chair to match, a brass fender in front of the fireplace and a china cabinet to hold my mother's 'best china', a set of delph that was still intact because we weren't allowed anywhere near it. Visitors could be safely shown in there because, as it wasn't lived in, it was always clean. My mother wouldn't dream of showing them into the kitchen, which had lino on the floor, where no two of anything matched, be it chairs, cups and saucers, or even knives and forks, and where toys would be strewn all over the floor. When guests were ushered into the spotless parlour my mother would always say, in the posh voice she reserved for the phone and for unexpected guests, 'I'm *turrably* sorry about the mess. It's *jost* so very hard to keep the house clean with children running all about the place.' Keeping up appearances was very important to Esther Cowan, and all the neighbours played the same game, giving the impression their house was spotless. You'd be hard pushed to find a speck of dust in their parlours, but they were always '*turrably* sorry about the mess'.

My mother was a brilliant mum, a whirlwind of activity, cooking, shopping and knitting for all of us. She'd start to knit a jumper while watching the six o'clock news, making Gerard or myself hold out an arm so she could measure the sleeve, and by the next morning we would have new jumpers going to Mass. She was a great cook, but she was a terrible dressmaker. This might not seem like an essential skill nowadays, but when clothes were expensive, most families made their own. It was just a pity Ma never managed to master the sewing machine! Gerard and I wore the strangest collection of shorts and trousers, not that it bothered us. We were probably more annoyed at having to wear matching outfits. Despite Esther's dislike of conformity, it was cheaper back then to buy four yards of one material than two each of different kinds. You didn't express your individuality in 1965!

Ma was not a sentimental woman, that's for sure. I've no memorabilia worth talking about from when I was young. A few photographs and that's it. I've asked friends if they, or their mother, had things like old school reports or baby teeth: they all have. I don't! And that's because my mother threw things out. If it couldn't be used any more, or if it was 'clogging up the place', as she put it, it was thrown in the bin.

I can still remember my mother bringing Maeve, my sister, to get her first haircut. Maeve must have been about one and a half or two years old. She had lovely blonde hair with natural curls at the back of her head. When he had finished, the hairdresser picked up the curls from the floor, put them in a box and said, 'Mrs Cowan, you should take these as a memory of your daughter's first haircut.'

My mother took the box of curls and in her posh voice she said, 'Oh that's very thoughtful of you. How very kind.'

After Maeve's haircut, we were going to Auntie Eileen's in Rathfarnham for our weekly visit and my mother opened the box to show it to Eileen. 'Wasn't that nice of the hairdresser to do that?' she said. 'He told me those curls would make a lovely keepsake. Here, Eileen, throw them in your bin. Will we go down to the shops and get the makings of a salad? We don't want to be eating a hot meal on a day like this.'

I suppose that with five people – two adults and three children (me, my brother Gerard, and Maeve), and a boxer dog, Rusty, living in a small two-up two-down Corporation house in Ballyfermot, there was just no room to be keeping mementoes of anything. We always joke that, of the three of us, Gerard was the only child who was actually planned. I was born on 15 July 1959, when my parents were staying with my auntie Eileen and uncle Harry. My parents were on the housing list, but to get a council house you had to have two children, which is why Gerard is only 18 months younger than me! He was born on 2 February 1961, and Maeve came along in 1965. We were thrilled to have a baby sister. When she was two months old, she became seriously ill and had to spend a year in hospital. None of us knows what the illness was – in those days you never spoke about this kind of thing – but I remember going to see her with Ma and Da and Gerard, and waving at her through the glass – we weren't allowed to get close to her, presumably because of the risk of infection.

Ma often used to tell me stories about my birth, in the Coombe hospital in Dolphin's Barn. According to my mother, a Traveller woman who was in the same ward, having her baby, told her that I'd grow up to be a very lucky person with a charmed life. For many years later, every time I got into any sort of trouble, my mother never failed to mention how the woman had got that wrong.

When I was born, it wasn't the done thing for fathers to be at the birth of their child. They either paced the hospital waiting room or went to the pub until the whole thing was over. So when my mother went in to give birth to me, her first child, Granny went to the hospital to be with her. And while my mother was waiting in bed for the labour to begin, she nervously asked her mother, 'What's it like, having a baby?'

My granny had given birth to seven children and had another seven miscarriages, so who better to advise her youngest daughter. Granny replied, 'Well, you won't spit it out, that's for sure. You'll know all about it soon enough, but when you're having it, make sure you don't show us up by screaming and shouting. Because if you do, I'll give you a good kick in the arse.'

Five hours later, in the early hours of the morning of July 15, the nurse was trying to get my mother to give one final push, and my mother was screaming blue murder, when Granny announced: 'Esther, I think it's time for that kick in the arse now.' And with that, my mother and Granny burst out laughing. She told me that that was the sound that greeted me when I came into the world. God knows what the nurse thought.

When I was two days old, I was whisked off to be baptised in a church around the corner from the hospital, St Nicholas of Myra, in Francis Street. Back in those days, babies were baptised as soon as possible after they were born in case they died without being christened, in a state of original sin, which meant they wouldn't be able to go straight to heaven. Instead, they would be sent to limbo, where they were to stay until the end of time. So, while we were all whisked off to be baptised, my mother missed all three of our christenings, being still in hospital recovering.

Years later, the Catholic Church changed its views on limbo and babies didn't have to be baptised so soon after being born, so much so that many years later when my sister Maeve had her first baby, Cian, my father would continually ask, 'When is she going to have that child baptised? He's six months old.' When Cian was eventually christened, he was nearly one year old and was walking. He kicked the priest when the holy water was poured on his head.

But back to my christening. I was named Rory, after my dad. It was a tradition in Ireland at the time that the first son was named after the father. My second name was a different story altogether. Because I was born on a holy day, Saint Swithin's Day, the priest gave all babies born on that day, who were christened in that church, the middle name of Mary. I suppose it could have been worse – I could have been Rory Swithin! However, needless to say I grew up hating that middle name and anytime anyone asked what it was, I always said Patrick, not Mary. Thinking of my real middle name, I was often reminded of the Johnny Cash song, 'A Boy Named Sue', where the character in the song goes off to search the honky-tonks and bars to kill the man who gave him that awful name. I could identify with that song and I planned that, just like Johnny Cash, I'd hunt that priest down and tell him that he was about to meet his maker. But I digress!

Back to the keepsakes. As soon as we got too old to play with a toy it got thrown in the bin. Sentimental value meant nothing to Esther Cowan. 'I don't want to be tripping over all your old rubbish,' she'd say indignantly when I asked her where a toy was that I couldn't find. 'If you left it where it's supposed to be, it must be there. If not, I probably threw it out.' She'd always say, 'I *probably* threw it out,' rather than admitting that she had.

I did learn one big lesson from her, though, and one which I still adhere to today: I cherished records and would take great care of them. I cleaned them just before I played them and kept them in their paper sleeves when they weren't being played. I never left them lying around. They were always kept in a record holder that could hold fifty singles. To this day, I look after my records and keep them in cases and I still regularly clean them. My records were my pride and joy, and my mother encouraged my interest. On rainy days, or days when it was too cold to go out to play, she'd often say, 'C'mon Rory, get your coat. Let's go into town to see if there's any new records we might like.' We would go into Dolphin Discs on Capel Street and she would stand there for hours while I browsed the charts and asked the man behind the counter to play the new Sandie Shaw or Cilla Black or Lulu or Dusty Springfield single. Pure bliss! Years later, I realised it was not about the records. It was about spending time together.

My passion for music must have begun early, because another vivid memory I have is of singing on the yellow painted swing that my father made for me, in the back garden. I was always singing when I was a child. A particular favourite was The Beatles' 'She Loves You'. I only knew the chorus and I'd sing it non-stop. It must have driven my mother and our neighbours mad.

On one side of our house, in number 63, were the McGarrys. Thomas McGarry and his sister Anne were best friends of mine, and their mother, Annie, was one of my mother's best friends. At the time, Mrs McGarry's mother, Mrs

Houlihan, lived with them and when I'd sing the chorus of 'She Loves You' one time too many, she'd shout out of the back window: 'Rory, sing "The Young Ones"!' Again, I didn't know the full Cliff Richard song, just the first four lines, but for a while it was a welcome change from 'She Loves You'. Eventually, when Mrs Houlihan was sick and tired of me singing the first four lines of 'The Young Ones' over and over again, she'd call me in to her. She'd be sitting beside the window, drinking a bottle of Guinness. 'Here, son,' she'd say, 'that singing is thirsty work. Have a sup of Guinness.' So I'd take a mouthful of Guinness from her bottle and she'd send me out the front to play on the street, where I wouldn't be inclined to sing.

Children were not only allowed a sup of drink in the early sixties, they were encouraged. A drop of Guinness in the morning because 'It's good for you and it'll build you up and put hairs on your chest,' my mother would snap. I don't know how she got my sister to drink it. I can't imagine little Maeve would have wanted hairs on her chest. Then there was a hot whiskey if you had a heavy cold or the flu. A glass of TK red lemonade would be boiled up in a pot, then a drop of whiskey and two spoons of sugar were added. 'That'll sweat the flu out of you. Now drink it while it's hot,' my mother would say authoritatively, 'because it won't do you any good if you let it go cold.' To this day, I can't drink Guinness or whiskey. I hate the smell of both and the idea of drinking them turns my stomach.

Thanks to my mother, music continued to be a huge part of my life, which led to my decision, aged eight, to marry

Sandie Shaw. Sandie had won the Eurovision Song Contest earlier that year with 'Puppet on a String', and I was in love with her. She was the most glamorous, most stylish woman I had ever seen. Now, I'd only ever seen her on the telly, but I was convinced that if I got to meet her, she would naturally fall in love with me. My mother had always told me, 'You're one in a million' and 'I'd be lost without you' when I was a small child, so maybe that's where I got the notions! (Now, in the autumn of 1967, that was changing: she was more likely to say, 'What did I do to deserve such a bold child as you?' I wasn't a natural troublemaker: it was just that trouble seemed to follow me around. At eight years of age I was a 'sensitive' little boy. I didn't know what that meant, but I'd heard my auntie Eileen saying it in a phone conversation to some friend of hers. Over the next year or two, if an adult asked what my name was, I'd say, 'I'm Rory, I'm a sensitive boy. Pleased to meet you.' This was met with guffaws of laughter, and I couldn't understand what they were laughing at.)

I could visualise our wedding very clearly. Sandie and I would get married in my local church, the Church of Our Lady of the Assumption, at the roundabout on Kylemore Road. I'd wear my Communion suit, which still fitted me a year later, though I would have preferred the suit to have had long trousers, not the short ones that only reached halfway down my thighs. Sandie's dress would be acres of white chiffon. There'd be thousands of people outside the church to cheer us and throw confetti and to wish us well as we set off on our honeymoon – a fortnight in a caravan in Rush, County Dublin. When we came back from our honeymoon at the seaside, we'd move in with my family on Kylemore Drive and we'd stay there until we got a house of our own on the same road. I knew Sandie had a house in London, which would come in handy if we wanted to travel from city to city. And as I'd be a married man, I wouldn't have to go to school any more. It was a perfect plan.

Picking the right priest to marry us was very important. I didn't want our parish priest to perform the ceremony because his sermons at Mass went on too long; I wanted a priest who galloped through the Mass. Father Matthew was my preferred option. If you were lucky enough to go to one of his Masses, you'd be out in half an hour. I decided the best place to ask him was at confession. At least we wouldn't be interrupted there. So, one Friday afternoon, on the way home from school, I went into the church and joined the queue at the confession box. When it was my turn, I went in, knelt down, and began: 'Bless me Father, for I have sinned; it's been a week since my last confession ...' And then I reeled off a few sins that I'd committed: 'I hit my younger brother, I was cheeky to my mother, I didn't do my homework and I got into trouble in school.' And then I said, 'Can you do me a favour, Father? I don't know the day yet, but when I do, I was wondering if you'd marry me and Sandie Shaw?'

I could hear him sniggering behind the grille and, after a moment or two, he said, 'When Miss Shaw agrees to marry you, then I'll be happy to perform the ceremony. Now tell me, my child, what's your name?'

What else could I do? I told the truth. After all, nobody would want to commit a sin by telling lies in the confession box. I said, 'My name is Rory and I'm a sensitive boy.' He spluttered so hard I didn't know whether he was laughing or having a heart attack. Then he composed himself and told me to say three Hail Marys and an Our Father for my penance and when I finished my Act of Contrition, he added, 'You should play football and you wouldn't be so sensitive.'

Everything was in place for the wedding. Getting a priest to marry us was the last link in the chain. Now, all I had to do was tell my mother. I walked slowly home, going over in my head how I was going to break the news to her. I decided the best way was to just tell her straight.

When I got home, she said, 'You're late. What have you been up to?'

When I told her I'd been to confession, she said, 'Did you confess that you were cheeky to me?' I told her I did. 'Good,' she said, 'I bet the priest was shocked to hear that. What penance did he give you? Five decades of the rosary, was it?'

'No, he only gave me three Hail Marys and one Our Father,' I said.

'What?' she screeched. 'For giving me cheek, he only gave you that? Being cheeky to your mother is a mortal sin. They mustn't have told him in the seminary. Giving cheek upsets Jesus in heaven. You made Jesus cry, you heathen. So, you think on that, the next time you decide to talk back to me.'

Ma would defend us to the death, but she was an unbelievable disciplinarian. If you were bold – if you answered back – you'd have to make sure you weren't near her, or anything she had to hand. If there was a tea towel, she'd flick it at us and that would be fine. If you were at the table, she'd reach across and you'd get the back of her hand. If you were near the fire, she'd pick up the poker – you'd never be bold when she was sitting by the fire! I used to see kids ignoring their mother when she called them, but there was no way I'd do that with mine. If she said, 'Rory, come here,' I would. I used to get the most disciplining. Maeve, my sister, was always good. She learned Irish and became a teacher – she was brilliant in school. As I got older, I got into all the trouble without even trying.

'Ma,' I said now, 'I've something to tell you.'

She gave me 'The Look', that stern glare that mothers reserve for their children. 'I knew it,' she said. 'You are in trouble. What have you done now?'

'Nothing, Ma. I'm getting married,' I said.

Well, that news made her chuckle. 'And who are you going to marry? Is it Ann McGarry?'

'No, Ma, Ann is just a friend. I'm going to marry Sandie Shaw,' I said.

Her chuckle became a cackle and her cackle became loud, convulsive laughter. I wished I knew what was so funny. When I told her that Father Matthew had agreed to marry Sandie and me her mood changed again.

'You didn't tell him where you live, did you?' she said, in the voice of a woman dreading the worst. 'Mother of God! Please tell me you didn't tell him whose child you are! I hope you didn't make a show of me in front of the priest.'

When I convinced her I had only told the priest my first name and didn't give him any other personal details, apart from my sins, she relaxed. 'Oh, wait till your father gets home. We'll see what he has to say,' she said, chuckling again.

Later that evening my da came home from work. 'Wait till you hear this,' Ma said to him. She paused for a moment to settle herself comfortably on a kitchen chair. 'Tell him,' she said to me. 'Tell him your big news.'

Drawing myself up to my full height and standing arrow straight, I said, 'I'm going to marry Sandie Shaw.' He started to snort with laughter and said, 'At least you won't have to buy her shoes, seein' as she sings in her bare feet.' And with that both he and my mother continued chuckling together.

What do they know? I thought. I was only eight years of age, but I knew I was different. Mind you, I didn't realise until a few years later just how different I was. At eight, I was positive I was going to marry Sandie Shaw very soon, and if everyone else thought that was funny, well, let them laugh.

When I wasn't planning my marriage to Sandie Shaw, I was out on the road along with all the other kids, playing the endless games that we played in those days, when we'd be outside from morning until it grew dark: Relevio, Red Rover, Tip the Can and Kerbs, which involved throwing a ball at the kerb so that it would bounce back in just the right way. Ballyfermot was crowded and noisy and full of life. You couldn't be lonely in Ballyfermot. There were always aul wans shouting, kids everywhere. There was no such thing as not having friends, because there were so many of us. Most were from huge families. Mrs Kavanagh had thirteen children – in a two-bedroom house! She must have spent more time doing hard labour than a convict breaking rocks. All mothers who gave birth spent a week in hospital. My Ma said this was the only holidays Mrs Kavanagh ever got, and that's why she had so many babies! Another woman won Housewife of the Year in 1968 or so. It was a huge deal in the neighbourhood. She won it because she said that a woman who has a nice dinner for her husband and doesn't talk back to him was the perfect housewife. The feminists would be in an uproar about that!

It was a different time, and neighbourhood justice dealt with a lot of social problems. Everybody looked out for everybody else. Ma always used to say that she had the best neighbours in Ballyfermot. She would go into Annie McGarry's every day, out of the back door and over the fence into her garden and they'd sit in the kitchen, drinking cups of tea and chatting away. You never knocked or went in the front door – always the back. When we moved to Athlone and Limerick and then Dundrum, none of the neighbours did that and Ma missed it.

Because there was never any escape from the racket, when I was seven or eight years of age I would escape from the house in the early hours of the morning and go for a wander. I used to love walking around at four or five o'clock in the morning, but I was only a kid and if the guards had seen me, they'd have taken me into care. But I thought it was great. I used to go into the playground and play on the swings. I didn't have to queue for anything the way I normally did; I had the whole place to myself.

But my parents did eventually find out – sometimes when I came home Dad would be out on the road, running up and down, frantic. Eventually, I overheard them discussing it. 'We'll have to lock him in. We can't have him getting out in the middle of the night,' Ma said.

Da said, 'You can't lock him in the bedroom because if the house goes on fire, he won't be able to get out.' So they decided to lock all the rooms downstairs. I couldn't open the front door anyway, because the lock was too high up; but if there was a fire, we'd all still be able to get out.

Years later, when Ma had dementia, she was sitting downstairs and my brother, Gerard, who was living at home at the time and who was her full-time carer, said he was nipping upstairs to get something. 'Now, Ma,' he said, 'You don't have to shout for me, because I'll only be a second.' He ran upstairs and as he explained to me later, 'I was only gone a minute and a half and I came back downstairs and she was gone.'

'Ah, Jaysus,' he said to himself, 'she's gone walking. She can't have gone very far, because she's very slow on her feet.' He went out to look on the road. No sign. He ran around the house and into the bedroom and she wasn't there, but then he spotted her sitting down on the grass in the park. 'We're going to have to lock her in,' he told me.

Who'd have thought that fifty years later, the tables would be turned? Needless to say, we never locked her in, no more than she ever locked me in, but it's a sad reminder that life really does turn full circle sometimes.

My mother encouraged all three of us to read. In spite of her own lack of education, she was an avid reader, and she passed that on to her children. When she was a child, girls weren't encouraged to read, so if someone caught her with a magazine, it would be taken off her and thrown on the fire. As for books, if she got hold of one she'd have to hide it. Books were considered a waste of time for girls – they'd only be getting married and all their reading would go to waste; that was the logic.

When I started school, we used to go to the Church of Adam and Eve in the city centre, where they had Ladybird books on spinners in the church shop, and I would be allowed to pick one, but the real excitement came with my first Famous Five book, *Five Run Away Together*. I'd never been so thrilled by a book in my life – imagine, five children going to an island to rescue a kidnapped girl! Another great place to get books was in Clerys department store, where they had a range of books in the children's department, like the Secret

Seven series, also by Enid Blyton, and the Bobbsey twins books, about a wealthy American family of two sets of twins, whom I found fascinating. The books were sixpence each, and the fare from Ballyfermot into town and back was threepence each way.

Ma would send Gerard and me into Clerys when we were around seven years of age, with strict instructions not to talk to anyone. As soon as I'd bought my book, I'd hurry off to the top of Parnell Square to read it in the Garden of Remembrance, then walk back down to the quays to get the bus home. I'd have two or three books on the go every week.

Recently I tweeted that I never throw books out, which is true – I have a big box of them up in the attic, and I mentioned a 1978 book of poems by Pam Ayres that I'd come across while sorting through papers one day. The next thing I knew, she'd replied! I nearly passed out. She composed the following poem, which makes me smile every time I see it:

Dear Rory,
That's a scene traumatic;
Books in boxes, in the attic,
Books like to be seen and read,
So, bring 'em all downstairs instead.
Display them in your happy home,
(Even that Pam Ayres's tome)
And if there is too large a crop
Take 'em down the Oxfam shop.

My mother was very careful about 'language'. 'Profanity has no place in polite conversation,' she'd say in her posh voice. 'If you have to use bad language, it just shows that you don't have the vocabulary to string a sentence together.' However, when I was a child, I used to embarrass my mother by saying the wrong things at the wrong times – including bad language. I could be sitting there quietly and then I'd say something without thinking and BOOM! 'Jesus, Mary and Joseph!' she'd scream. 'Why do you always show me up?' I couldn't answer because I was trying my best to dodge her wallops as she ranted at me.

One Saturday, sometime in 1965, we were going to see *The Sound of Music* in the Classic Cinema, Terenure, a 1930s building directly opposite the synagogue – it's now a furniture showroom, I think. All my aunties on my mother's side of the family and my cousins were going to the 11 a.m. screening. So there was my mother and Gerard and myself, my aunties Eileen, Nancy, Josie and Mag, and my cousins Grainne, Paul, Mary and Patrick, all of whom still lived in the Rathfarnham area.

Now, going to the cinema in the 1960s was a big deal, one of the only ways of entertaining small kids on a rainy day. I can still remember the Sunday-afternoon children's matinee at the Gala Cinema in Ballyfermot: It was a real old fleapit of a place, but we loved it. Inside there'd be pandemonium, with kids charging around the place, fighting, throwing marbles, used sweet wrappers, plastic lemonade bottles and anything thing else that could be thrown at the screen. But the spitting competitions were the ones you definitely tried to avoid. And the only way to do that was to get a seat at the back of the stalls or at the back of the balcony. That way, when the spitting started, the golliers, as we used to call them, would be aimed towards the screen, so they could be seen in the projector light and would go right over our heads. Worst of all, every week some kid or other would think it'd be hilarious to pee over the balcony. The usherettes, as they were known back then, and the cinema manager would be angrily running about the cinema scanning the rows of children in an effort to stamp out any bad behaviour. It was the norm to see some child being dragged out of his or her seat screaming, 'It wasn't me, honest.'

The only time we behaved ourselves was when the films were being shown. There were usually two: the first was what we called 'a follyer-upper', in other words, an episode in a series, like *Zorro*, and each episode would have a cliff-hanger ending to encourage you to come back the following week. The main film would be either a Disney film or a recent western or light comedy. During both films, we'd all cheer the heroes and boo and hiss at the baddies. Between the two films came the ads and the mayhem would begin again.

The family outing to the Classic in Terenure to see the *The Sound of Music* was a much more sedate affair. It was also the highlight of my six-year-old life. I was engrossed in the film and totally oblivious to everything and everyone around me. I loved everything about it: the songs, the von Trapp children, the story, the nuns, Julie Andrews; it was the best film I had ever seen. Everything was tickety-boo until the part in the film where the von Trapp family are hiding from the Nazis behind the gravestones in the abbey. When they think it's safe to come out, they slowly emerge into the open. Now, at this point in the film, Rolf, who had joined the Nazi party, was returning to the crypt and the family were in danger of being discovered. As they emerged from behind the gravestones I screamed, 'Look out, you fucking eejits!' Suddenly I was aware of everyone in the cinema erupting with laughter and my mother dragging me out of the cinema by the scruff of the neck into the bright sunshine.

'Where did you hear language like that?' she screamed. 'Everyone in my family will be told about you. I won't be able to hold my head up in Rathfarnham again!' My one thoughtless comment meant that I didn't get to see the end of *The Sound of Music* until it came out on video over twenty years later.

THREE

Wonderful Christmastime

For someone who wasn't very sentimental, Esther went mad at Christmas. She complained about it being too commercialised and that the season started in November instead of December. 'By the time Christmas gets here, you'd be sick of it,' she used to protest. These days Christmas starts in August, as anyone who visits Brown Thomas in Grafton Street knows. Its top floor is completely turned over to Christmas, with trees, ornaments, decorations, Christmas-themed biscuits ... In August? Mary hasn't even told Joseph she's pregnant yet.

But Esther loved Christmas. Come December every year, she'd go all out to make this Christmas the best ever. And Christmas did sort of start in November for her. This was when the house had to be done up. New wallpaper for all the rooms, including the bathroom. A new matching set of toilet mat, bath mat and towels from Guiney's in Talbot Street. The front-room carpet would be 'shampooed', which meant my mother would spend half a day on her hands and knees, scrubbing it with a basin of carpet cleaner mixed with hot water. Every other room had lino and this would have to be polished until you could nearly see your face in it. Every evening for about a week, my father would come home from work, have his tea and immediately get on with painting the ceilings in every room and hanging the new wallpaper. I used to think all this activity was done so that Santy would see that our house was spotless when he came to deliver the toys. I could picture him taking a rest in our gleaming kitchen, and thinking to himself, 'Isn't this a lovely house?' while he was drinking his bottle of Guinness and eating the slice of Christmas cake we left out for him on the kitchen table.

But the whole Christmas rigmarole would start with the tree. It would be bought and brought home in early December. Like everything else that became a fixture in the home, my mother chose the tree. Bearing measurements of floor-to-ceiling heights, herself and Da would set off to buy it. After looking at dozens of trees, some too tall, some too small, some too sparse, some that weren't green enough, and getting my Da to hold up every tree with possibilities while she walked all around it and looked it up and down, she'd eventually decide on the perfect specimen. Then, at last, my father would be allowed tie it to the roof rack of the car and bring it home. And after deciding where it was to be perched – which turned out to be in the same spot as always – the real fun started.

Every year it was the same: Da would have to pare down the base of the tree so it would fit into the stand. The little hacksaw was retrieved from the toolbox and the carving knife was taken out of the cutlery drawer. Myself and my brother used to take bets on how long it would be before my father started cursing, usually after cutting his hand or getting pine needles in his eye, and we would be sent out of the room. As soon as we heard, 'That fuckin' tree,' my mother would whoosh myself and Gerard out the door with the instruction to 'Go out and play.'

That evening, we'd all decorate the tree. The baubles and fairy lights would be taken down from the attic and removed from the boxes and newspaper they'd been stored in since the previous Christmas. My father was Director of Operations. He had a routine. First the lights were hung on the tree. 'Watch where you're walking,' was a yearly command when it looked like myself or my brother were going to step on the lights, which were strewn across the floor after he managed to untangle them. When they were draped around the tree to my mother's satisfaction, then came the switching on of the lights. They never worked. This led to a frantic search of drawers and presses for the packet of spare bulbs. After the blown bulb had been identified and replaced, the lights would come on.

Then it was mine and Gerard's turn to get stuck in. We'd rush around the tree, sticking baubles on branches and throwing tinsel as high up the tree as we could. And when all that was done, my father would finish the whole thing off by putting the star on top. Years later, I found out that after we had gone to bed, my parents would take all the decorations down and start again. The thing was, myself and my brother could only reach about halfway up the tree, so the bottom half was fully decorated and the top half was bare. When we got up the next morning it never dawned on us that the tree looked very different from the way we had left it the night before.

Next on my mother's list was taking down from its shelf at the top of her wardrobe the cardboard box that held all the Christmas cards we'd received the year before. These were placed into two piles: cards from those still living; and cards from those who had died in the last year. Thankfully there was always more in the first pile than the second. The people who had sent her a Christmas card the previous year, and who were still alive, were the only ones getting a card from her this year; if she sent a card one year and the person she sent it to neglected to send her one in return, they were off her Christmas card list for the following year.

When Ma went through her Christmas cards, she would sit up half the night writing personal messages in each of them. It was never just 'Happy Christmas from Esther and family'. No, Esther Cowan had a personal message for every card. She used to send out about a hundred cards every year and we'd get roughly the same number back. Lengths of wool would be pinned to the walls and the chimney breast and the cards draped over them. This was one of the few ways my parents had of keeping in touch with all their friends and family living abroad. Like most people at that time, we didn't have a phone, so the only way of staying in touch was by sending and receiving letters or Christmas cards.

The first Saturday after 8 December, we would be brought to see Santa in Clerys department store. I thought the Clerys Santa was the best. We'd have to walk through Santa's toy factory and there'd be elves and helpers moving toys and parcels for Santa's sack. You'd get to see all the toys that were available that year. 'Just tell Santa you want a pair of skates and a surprise,' my mother would warn, if she saw my eyes popping with delight at some toy that cost a fortune.

The eighth of December used to be a huge shopping day in Dublin, because thousands upon thousands of people from down the country would come to the city to do their Christmas shopping. It was also around this day that the carol singers took to the streets. They'd soon wear out their welcome as far as my mother was concerned. She'd be rushing around trying to buy the Christmas things she wanted and she'd be slowed down by all these carol singers blocking the pavements. 'If I hear "Away In a Manger" once more they'll have me away in an asylum,' she'd say bitterly. I bet the shoplifters hated those carol singers too. I can just imagine them charging out of Roches Stores or Arnotts, bottles of aftershave and perfume stuck up their jumpers, security guards running after them, straight into a bunch of carol singers.

After we'd visited Santa and told him what we wanted for Christmas, we'd be brought to the café in Arnotts department store for a cream doughnut and a glass of orange. Every year, I'd deliberately get lost in the shop. I'd tell my mother I was going to the toilet, and while my brother and sister finished their cake and fizzy drink I'd hide out of sight until my mother realised I was still gone. She'd be panicking and rushing around the café looking for me, and I'd make my way to the information desk on the ground floor.

Back in the 1960s, Arnotts had a public address system with speakers all over the store. The girl at the information desk would read out the special offers that were on that day, or let the customers know what new lines had just come in. If a child was lost, she'd announce that too. I'd tell her that I was lost, give her my name, and she'd get on her Bing-Bong. 'A little boy has been lost,' her voice would boom from all the speakers in the store, as if she were giving a sermon. 'His name is Rory Cowan. Would his parent or parents please come to the information desk to collect him?' A few minutes later, Esther would come rushing down the stairs and across the shop, with my younger brother and sister running behind her. 'Oh, you're very kind,' she'd say gratefully to the girl behind the desk. Then she'd look at me and snarl through her teeth, 'Just you wait till I get you home.'

I loved hearing my name being called out over the PA system in Arnotts. I was fond of drama from an early age!

At least once a week during December, my mother used to say, 'I'm just dashing into town to get a few things I need for Christmas,' and she'd come home on the bus later that day laden down with shopping bags. The 'few things' she needed tended to be things that caught her eye and weren't really needed at all. 'I got these two bottles of perfume off a fella in Moore Street,' she'd tell Da. 'They'll come in handy if one of your aunties on your father's side drops over without letting me know first.'

She hated relations calling in without letting her know well in advance, so she could have the house gleaming and a nice spread ready for them, usually a salad with slices of ham and chicken. Whenever relations just popped in with a cheery greeting of 'We were just passing,' it was all she could do to hold her temper in.

We always knew she was annoyed because she'd put on her refined voice: 'You should have let me know you were coming,' she'd say with a note in her voice that was anything but welcoming. Then, smoothing out the creases in her apron, she'd continue: 'I'll just make you up a nice salad.' While she was saying this she'd be beckoning me with her eyes and a tilt of her head to tell me to go out to the hall. She'd come out with a 'Where is that paper boy? He's getting later and later every day. I'm going to have to cancel the delivery.' Then she'd take her purse out of her handbag and say, 'I'm going to pay him what's owed up to today and cancel my order.' We didn't actually get our papers delivered – it was all just a ruse. She'd give me a pound note, with whispered instructions to 'Get slices of ham and chicken, a half-dozen eggs, a jar of beetroot, a head of lettuce, six tomatoes and a bunch of scallions. Oh, and two pints of milk.' Closing her purse, she'd hiss, 'And if the insurance man or the television man calls this week, don't answer the door.' Like most people in Ballyfermot, we rented a television from RTV Rentals.

A while ago I got a letter from an insurance company with a statement for an account in my name and it dawned on me that it was one of these 'penny policies' that my mother paid into every week 'in case any of yous die', as she put it. She had started this policy for me just after my father died in 2008. She must have set up a direct debit to pay it out of her pension and the cost of servicing it was probably more than the policy. The value, almost nine years after she took it out, was €684.

'Doing the last of your Christmas shopping?' neighbours would ask when they saw my mother struggling up the road with armfuls of bags. 'Indeed,' Ma used to say wearily. 'I'm as broke as the Ten Commandments.' The women would laugh at that, even though they'd heard it, and said it, year in, year out. It would also give my mother a chance to talk to a neighbour and leave the shopping bags out of her sore hands for a few minutes, before she'd pick them up again and continue on her way back home. When she got home and unpacked everything, she'd realise she'd forgotten something or other, and that would be her excuse to go back into town in a few days' time. Waving her hand at all her shopping laid out on the table, she'd say, 'I didn't need any of this old rubbish. But the one thing I wanted, I forgot. Ah, well, I'll have to back again and get it,' which meant she'd an excuse for a further day of shopping for more rubbish she didn't need.

The Friday before Christmas, the tip list would be drawn up. This list consisted of the people who deserved to be 'looked after' at Christmas for all the work they did during the year: the bread man, the milkman, the bin man, the slop man – who collected your 'organic waste', as it would be called nowadays, to feed to pigs – the coal man, the postman, the lollipop lady and any number of others. The amount each was to get was written beside their name. They all had to get a tip so that they would continue looking after us the next year: if you didn't tip them, the chances were that the next year your empty bin would be dropped off anywhere except at your gate, or your post would be delivered to another address entirely.

All those Christmases at home in Ballyfermot seem to blend into each other now, humdrum memories of presents and visits and sweets that formed the backdrop to my life growing up. During the month of December, every year until my father died, the same jokes would be wheeled out. My mother would ask, 'Will I get my stocking filled this year?' My father would reply, deadpan: 'Oh, yeah, you will, with your bleedin' leg.' And the two of them would laugh heartily. Every Christmas Eve, after she'd prepared the turkey to be cooked the next morning, she'd say to my father, 'Okay, now I've plucked and stuffed it. All you have to do is kill it.' The pair of them would burst into peals of laughter.

After a few years of this, and as I got a year older each time Christmas came around, the little jokey things they said used to annoy me. It might have been funny the first time, I reasoned, but *every year*? But I get it now and the memories of those little in-jokes bring a smile to my face. It's weird the things you remember.

Come to think of it, I remember the day Judy Garland died in 1969, but I've no memory of the moon landing a few months later. I really wasn't going to be anything else but gay, was I?

FOUR

I Wish

I can still remember my first day at school in September 1964. I bawled my eyes out. I couldn't believe that my mother was making me go to school and that she was leaving me *by myself* in a classroom. Ma was always there when I was growing up, and I couldn't understand why she wasn't just outside. When I was in hospital getting my tonsils out – which wasn't long after starting school – she'd said, 'I'll be sitting outside – don't be worrying.' I was in hospital for four days, and I believed she was sitting outside in the corridor all the time.

The schoolroom had a big sandpit in the corner – it was a play centre, really, and the teacher, Miss Lally, was gorgeous – she looked like a real sixties girl – but I cried my eyes out all the way there. Dad was in knots trying to suppress his laughter at my histrionics and Ma kept saying, 'I'll be in here with you. Just outside.' Of course, I kept telling the teacher, 'I'm going out to see my Ma. She's just outside.' And she'd have to tell me that it wasn't time yet. School finished at 12.30 p.m. for the first week and it felt like the longest three and a half hours ever. I couldn't believe it went on for so long. I hated it. At the end of the week I said to my mother, 'I'm not going back any more.'

She laughed and said sarcastically, 'No problem, I'll let you stay at home, because I love spending every waking moment picking up after you.'

'Do you mean it?' I asked hopefully.

'What do you think?' she snapped. 'You're going to school.'

I went to bed that night, dreading getting up the next morning, and for that first week I cried and cried and cried, then one day I said to myself, 'What on earth are you crying for?' I realised I was actually enjoying it. I made great friends and had a good time. Ballyfermot National School and the secondary school next door were recognised as the biggest in Europe at the time, 1964. There were at least forty kids in each class. There were gangs of kids, so if you wanted to join in in anything, you could. If you wanted to be on your own, you could become invisible. I'd walk home for lunch every day along the main road with all the other hordes of kids, Thomas and Anne McGarry walking home with me. Everyone did – you walked. Dad would drive me to school at the beginning, but after that, we walked. In Athlone, the school was further away, so my parents got me a bike!

We had the lovely Miss Lally for junior infants, or 'low babies' as it was called at the time, then high babies, or senior infants, and after that, first class, where we were taught by Sister Catherine. I remember poor old Sister Catherine very well. She always seemed to get the wrong end of the stick. It was all to do with how she disciplined the six- and seven-year-old boys in her care, which, as you can imagine, was no easy task.

Unlike most of the other teachers, Sister Catherine never hit children. This lovely little old nun, who couldn't have been more than five feet tall, never slapped them, or gave them six of the best on the knuckles with the side of a ruler. She had her own way of dishing out punishments. If a boy was talking when he shouldn't have been, she'd put gaffer tape over his mouth. If he was fidgeting, she'd gaffer-tape his hands to the side of the desk. And if he was away from his desk without her permission, she'd gaffer-tape his ankles to the legs of the desk. These punishments would last about five minutes and when she removed the tape she'd say, 'Have you learned your lesson?'

'Yes, Sister.'

'Well, don't do it again.'

Back in the mid-sixties there was no Childline. Try gaffer-taping a child now and you'll end up in court. But to us children back then, getting gaffer-taped by Sister Catherine was more a game than a punishment. We loved the attention we got from classmates when we shrugged our shoulders or acted out not being able to speak or move our arms or legs. It was almost like our games of cowboys, where someone was captured and tied to a lamp post until he was able to escape.

However, things took a nasty turn one day. Mark Williams must have been talking out of turn, fidgeting, and away from his desk, because Sister Catherine had him tied up like a hostage in 1980s Beirut. His mouth had a strip of gaffer tape over it and his arms and ankles were taped to the side and legs of the desk. This was just the calm before the storm. About two minutes into his punishment, who should arrive up at the class but his mother. She'd come down to the school to bring her son the lunch he'd forgotten to take with him when he was leaving the house that morning.

The classroom door was a heavy wooden door with a long thin pane of glass down the side, so the head nun, or other teachers, could see inside without having to disturb the class. Mrs Williams looked in through this pane of glass to see where her child was, and when she saw him, all tied up and with gaffer tape over his mouth, her face froze in shock. Then, with a scream of 'Me child!', she barged into the classroom and with arms wide open, ran to where Mark was sitting and ripped the tape off his mouth. 'What happened?' she screeched.

Mark Williams got as far as 'The nun …' when all hell broke loose. Mrs Williams turned around and grabbed Sister Catherine with one hand while she punched her again and again with the other. 'Why don't you pick on someone your own size, ya fat bitch?' she said, as she laid into her.

None of us children could believe what we were seeing. We had always been taught to be a deferential to priests and nuns, so to see a woman of the cloth being battered was astonishing. And Mrs Williams could have given Wonder Woman a run for her money. She dragged the veil and wimple off Sister Catherine and threw the nun to the floor.

We were in shock when we saw Sister Catherine's hair. We all thought that women had their heads shaved when they became nuns. 'They love God and that's why they're baldy, so no man will fancy them. God likes his wives to be baldy,' was the word on the street among the kids. So we were amazed to see that not only was Sister Catherine not bald, but she had quite thick short brown hair. That she had a head full of hair was of more interest to us than the fact that she was being beaten up. Most of us had seen women fighting on the streets before, so we weren't bothered by that so much, but a nun with hair? That was a revelation.

'You'd better not be in trouble with the police,' my mother ranted when I arrived home that afternoon, banging on the knocker and out of breath. I couldn't wait to tell her what had happened that morning. She listened to my story, then said Mrs Williams was common. 'And don't you repeat that outside this house,' she snapped. It was always very important to my mother that we 'never repeat anything you hear in this house'. Once, I remember her telling my aunty Eileen about something I'd said outside that had caused her mortification. 'Did he misquote you?' Eileen asked. 'No, he bloody didn't,' Esther said, her voice going up a couple of octaves. 'He repeated word for word what I shouldn't have said in the first place.'

My mother also had a great suspicion of people knowing our business. Another of her phrases was: 'Don't ever let me see you in the paper.' What she would have thought about social media and reality TV is anyone's guess: in those days, people lived in fear of having their name publicised, because it meant they'd done something wrong, even committed a crime.

I could always make my mother laugh. For a while, I never knew why she was laughing at something I said or did, and it used to bother me, because as far as I was concerned, I wasn't trying to be funny. That all changed the year I turned eight and was in first class. That was when I learned I could get away with murder if I told my mother a funny story. Again, Sister Catherine was the star of the show. She'd been preparing us for the religious rite of first Communion, walking up and down the aisles between the desks, instructing us on the importance of the Communion rite, how to make our first confession and the significance of the Communion wafer, which would bring us closer to Jesus.

Then she suddenly stopped at Mickey Dowling's desk. Her eyebrows shot up and her voice went up about six octaves. 'Michael Dowling, just look at the dirt on your hands. And your nails are filthy. And your face and neck. You didn't wash yourself before you came to school this morning, did you?' Without waiting for an answer, she continued: 'And I'm sure you could grow potatoes in the dirt in your ears.'

Mickey Dowling's face was as red as a tomato and the rest of the class were sniggering at his embarrassment. Sister Catherine, shaking her head in mock disgust, said, 'Michael, you must wash yourself properly before you come to school. You're not a ragamuffin or an urchin, so you shouldn't look like one. When you get up in the morning, you make sure you give your hands and face and neck a good wash before you come to school.' With that, she went back to explaining the importance of our first Holy Communion.

Needless to say, Mickey Dowling was tormented for the rest of the day by everyone in the class. He was ridiculed about being filthy and we wouldn't allow him to play with us during the morning break. Kids can be very cruel at that age. But it was only short term; by the next day, we would have moved on to someone else to tease, each one of us delighted it wasn't our turn.

However, poor Mickey was more upset than any of us realised, and when he went home he told his mother every detail of his day. We all knew that Mrs Dowling suffered from her 'nerves' and that the slightest thing could set her off, and when she did go off on one the whole street could hear her.

When Mr Dowling came home from work later that evening, he found his very distressed wife and son waiting for him and no dinner on the table. So, to calm the pair down, and in the hopes of getting his dinner, he promised that he'd go down to the school in the morning and have a word with the nun and sort everything out.

The next morning, just after school started and we had all said our morning prayers – three Hail Marys, an Our Father and a Glory Be to the Father – there was a knock on the door. Mr Dowling, who was on his way to work in Hammond Lane foundry, had come to see Sister Catherine. He came in, walked straight up to Sister Catherine and said in a loud, gruff voice: 'Sister, did you say my Mickey was dirty?'

There was a pause of about a second and then the class of forty-three children erupted with laughter. Everyone except Mickey Dowling, that is. He just crossed his arms on his desk and buried his head in them with embarrassment. The rest of us couldn't believe what we had just heard and as we howled with laughter, Mr Dowling looked at the class as if he wanted the ground to open up and swallow him. He looked at Sister Catherine, who hadn't a clue what had just happened, and said, 'Sorry, Sister' and kept repeating 'Sorry, Sister' as he walked slowly backwards, twisting his cap in his hands, until he had left the classroom.

As you can imagine, I couldn't wait to get home to tell my mother what had happened, and when the lunch break came, I ran all the way. Because I ran home and didn't dawdle as I sometimes did, my mother looked at me suspiciously when she opened the door.

'You're home early. What have you done?' she asked.

'Nothing, Ma,' I replied, as I ran past her. 'Wait till I tell you what happened in school today.'

'Wash your hands first before you sit down at that table.'

I went to the sink to wash my hands, while my mother put a sandwich on the table, poured me a glass of milk, and herself a cup of tea, and said, 'Right, start at the beginning.'

I gave my mother a blow-by-blow account. When I told her about nobody playing with Mickey during the break, she said, 'Ah, the poor little sod.' And with that, she gave me a dagger stare. 'I hope you weren't one of those boys bullying him?' Being a bully was, in my mother's book, beyond the pale.

'No, Ma, listen,' I said.

When I got to the part about Mr Dowling storming into the class, Ma commented, 'I'd say it very nearly gave the poor nun a heart attack, that big lump barging in like that. What did he do then?'

When I told her the punchline, my mother spat out the mouthful of tea she was drinking and burst out laughing. For a moment, both of us were howling with laughter. Then almost as if someone had flicked a light switch, she stopped, as if she realised what we were doing. 'You get yourself down to confession,' she said sternly, 'and you tell the priest you used bad language in front of your mother.' With that, she stood up and said, 'I've to pop in to see Mrs McGarry. You finish your lunch and get straight down to that chapel.' It didn't dawn on her that I hadn't even made my first confession at that point and I thought it better not to tell her.

Five minutes later, through the open windows, I could hear both women screaming with laughter as my mother repeated the story of Mr Dowling's 'dirty mickey'. And it dawned on me that if I could tell a funny story, or be the class clown, I wouldn't get picked on in school. After all, nobody will hit you if they're laughing.

I didn't get up to mischief too often when I was a child, but I did start smoking when I was eight, though I didn't inhale until years later. All the kids my age were smoking, so I thought I'd join them. Thankfully, these days smoking isn't cool, but at that time in Ballyfermot you didn't want to be the odd one out or you'd get picked on. So I joined the gang. In those days schoolchildren were expected to bring a penny into school every week 'for the black babies', especially during Lent. The term 'black babies' has fallen from use now, thank God, and my father used to despise it. He was ahead of his time in that respect. He hated any phrases that were offensive, or that singled out groups of people, such as Travellers, as being different. You can imagine what he made of the term 'black babies' being used to encourage aid to Africa, but he would still cough up the penny every time I asked for it.

I have to point out, however, that the poor babies of Africa never got anything from me after I started smoking. There was a man on Kylemore Road, on the way to school, who had a stall selling sweets, bottles of lemonade, crisps and cigarettes. At the time you could buy loose cigarettes – one, two, three, right up to a packet of ten. For a penny, I could buy two loose cigarettes: I'd smoke one on the rest of the way to school and share it among my friends; and we'd smoke the other at the back of the sheds during the morning break. By the time you got to the end of a smoke, it'd be soggy from the saliva of all the kids who'd shared it, but we didn't care. We thought smoking made us grown-up and we thought we were cool.

During Lent in 1967 or 1968 there was a scheme in our school to name a baby in Africa if you brought in enough money. It was basically sponsoring a child and you could write letters to him or her and they could write back to you. Looking back it was a terrible idea, racist to its core. It assumed that women in Africa were so backward that they wouldn't even think to give names to their babies. Now, I cringe when I recall that I had called mine Napoleon Solo from *The Man from U.N.C.L.E.*

In the sixties boys went to an all-boys' school after their first Communion, so off we went, to be taught by Brother Cyprian, or Zippo, as we called him. He was very well known in the area as an animal who battered kids. Apart from Sister Catherine, Miss Lally had been our teacher until then. I couldn't believe the change that came with moving across the road. One particular incident brought the new reality home to me.

I loved the Eurovision Song Contest and this year, 1968, Cliff Richard had sung the UK's entry, 'Congratulations', and he'd lost out on winning by one point. (This was in the days when they entered real pop stars in the competition.)

The following Monday in school, Brother Cyprian came in. We said prayers first, then he said, 'Did anyone see the Eurovision Song Contest?' A whole lot of hands shot up and he added: 'And Cliff Richard beaten by one point.' We were thinking that it was great – and so unusual – that we weren't getting straight down to work as we usually did. 'Does anyone know the song?' Brother Cyprian said, and, of course, my hand shot up. I was called up to stand in front of the class and opened my mouth to sing the first couple of lines of the song – and then everything went dark. The punch in the face he'd given me threw me right across the classroom. When I came to, I was holding on to the radiator at the other side of the room. It was the first time I'd literally seen stars – white dots that got bigger and bigger in front of my eyes. I staggered up, thinking, 'Why is he hitting me? I sang the right words.'

'How dare you sing the English song in the song contest, when you should have been singing the Irish one?' I didn't understand what I'd done wrong: all I had done was sing the song, just as he'd asked me. I went back to my seat and sat down, head throbbing. When I went home that afternoon, Ma noticed my black eye. 'What happened to you?' she said.

'The Brother hit me.'

'What did he hit you for?' she said, and when I told her, she just said, 'Right, sit down and have your tea. I'll sort it out tomorrow.'

'No, Ma, it's all right,' I protested. There was no way I wanted her to go into tackle Brother Cyprian. A similar thing had happened to a neighbour's child. He'd been punched by a Brother and had come home and told his older brother, who'd gone down to the school and had knocked seven bells out of the man. After that, the boy was left sitting there for the rest of primary school and they never asked him a question or if he had his homework done: they just ignored him. He was getting bored and he'd misbehave and wouldn't study in school. From eight years of age. Depriving him of his education was a dreadful punishment for a kid, and I didn't want a taste of it.

'No,' she insisted. 'Leave it to me.' I knew that my mother was a force to be reckoned with. If we stepped out of line, we'd know about it, but if any one of us had been wronged, she would defend her children to the hilt. She went down the following day, walked straight into the classroom and told Brother Cyprian, 'I want to talk to you now.' Something in her tone told him that he'd better listen. 'I'm his mother and he told me what you did to him yesterday.'

Brother Cyprian busied himself making excuses that it wasn't that bad and that Ma wasn't to be worrying, but she said, 'For a start, this wasn't a slap, or a tap with a ruler, it was a punch in the face, and I'm not having that. If he'd been misbehaving, I wouldn't have minded you chastising him, but he didn't do anything wrong. He did exactly what you asked him to do.'

He kept trying to play it down and eventually she said to him, 'May you never see the gates of heaven after what you've done to my boy.'

Well, his face drained of colour. 'Ma'am, please don't say that.'

'I will say it,' she insisted. 'May you never see the gates of heaven for what you're after doing to children.' It was like putting a curse on someone, to wish that they not see the gates of heaven, and it was said very rarely in those days, when faith was so important.

Years later, Ma told me that she thought she'd have to move me to another school, fearful of what might happen to me because of what she'd done – but it worked, because he never hit me again. That was the way things were in my day. I wasn't aware of any sexual abuse when I was at school, but physical abuse was very much part of the picture. If it hadn't been for my mother, I'm sure it would have happened a lot more. I remember, years later, asking her why she paid almost daily visits to the school when I was a child. It used to embarrass me, when I'd see her approaching, shopping bags in her hands, because it looked like she was an overprotective mother and there was no way I wanted to give the other kids an excuse to tease me. Every time, there was a different pretext: 'Rory is having problems with his maths. He was telling me last night that he couldn't keep up ...' Whatever excuse she invented, she'd make it clear to the priest that she knew exactly what was going on during my school day. As she explained to me, 'Rory, at the time we were all aware of the rumours about what was going on with the priests and the only thing I could do to protect you was to let them know that you spoke to me about *everything*.' I was in awe of just how far Ma was prepared to go to protect me and my siblings. I feel very lucky.

Brother Cyprian also taught the accordion and gangs of people learned it at the time. David Dawson was a good friend of mine and he played the instrument, so I wanted to learn and my mother agreed for some reason – this must have been before the Eurovision incident. The class was held in what looked like one of the old football changing rooms. All the kids were sitting in a line, playing some song on their accordions, while the brother walked up and down with a big leather strap, whacking them on the side of the head if they played a wrong note or chord. I thought to myself, Are you mad, Rory? There's no way you're doing this.

Mam was delighted I'd said no in the end, because accordions weren't cheap, but I did learn the guitar later, when we moved to Limerick for a couple of years. I went to the Crescent Comprehensive in Dooradoyle, which was run by Jesuits who were all rugby mad. I loved it, because they taught technical drawing and our school up in Dublin didn't have that, but the Jesuits insisted that I play rugby, and I refused. Can you see me playing rugby?! I did try it once. I stood shivering with cold, as far away from the action on the pitch as I could get. But then the ball somehow ended up near me and, to my horror, two teams of hulking great rugby players were charging in my direction. So what could I do? I took to my heels and didn't stop running until I got to the changing rooms, got dressed, sneaked out of school, got the bus home and told my mother in no uncertain terms that I was never going to play rugby.

Ma tried to encourage me, saying, 'You'll enjoy it once you get used to it,' but I had no interest in rugby or football and eventually my mother went down to the school and said, 'He won't play, can you give him anything else to do?' They couldn't find anything else for me to do on a Wednesday afternoon, but I said I'd learn the guitar, so Dad bought me one. He was great like that, Da – always ready to encourage us.

I used to go to this man in Limerick and I was strumming along with him, thinking that I'd learn to play like Marc Bolan or Jimi Hendrix after one or two lessons. The next thing he said, 'Sing along with this,' and he began to play 'Michael Row the Boat Ashore', a very gentle folk hymn. I couldn't believe it. What happened to Jimi Hendrix? He explained that I needed to walk before I could run, but I thought, No way. I hadn't got the patience for that! On the way home I had to cross the Shannon and I stood on the bridge for a moment before tossing the guitar in. I can still see it floating downstream. I didn't breathe a word to my parents and they never noticed that the guitar was missing, but every now and then, they'd ask, 'How are you getting on with the guitar?' I'd tell them that it was all fine.

Now all I had to do was find something else to do on my Wednesday afternoons off school, so I used to go to the pictures. There were only four cinemas in the city at the time, and I visited all of them. I was only thirteen and was completely unsupervised. Anything could have happened, and the films could be for over-18s, but nobody checked. I thought it was great. I had every Wednesday afternoon free – what could be better?

This might surprise you, but I had a great time at school. I always followed my own path. Just as I threw the guitar away, if I didn't want to do anything, I didn't do it. I've always thought that if you don't do what you like, you'll always feel there's something else out there.

When we moved to Athlone, when I was ten years old, I went to the Marist Brothers, but I remember it mostly because it was the first time I went on stage. I loved it. I was only at the school for two years, but I had the lead role in both annual plays – I remember playing the part of King Cornelius, whoever he was! I was tall even then, so I always played the grown-up.

The only time I ever got nervous on stage was on my very first night on *Mrs Brown's Boys*, and then only because I was the last-minute replacement for the original Rory. Even then, arenas with audiences of ten thousand people never fazed me. I couldn't wait to get out there. Every actor talks about their dark side and that they're depressed when off stage. I just went on, had a great time, tried my best and that was that.

Recently, I put a photo of me in the Marist Brothers school up on Facebook, asking if anyone could remember Brother Anthony, because he was the best teacher I ever had, even if he did annoy my mother by telling her that I was average! I got lots of responses from past pupils and I found out that after teaching my class, he'd left the brotherhood (I don't think we drove him to it!), got married, had two children and moved away. Brother Anthony couldn't have been further removed from Brother Cyprian – he was a great teacher, who always encouraged us. I can still remember the raffles and sponsored walks he'd organise for the Church. He came from Sligo town and every so often he'd drive a busload of us up to Sligo, park somewhere in the town and say, 'Off you go. I'll be back here at five o'clock to take you home,' and we'd scatter. He was probably going off to visit his family. From half ten in the morning until five o'clock in the evening, we'd sell the tickets around the town, then we'd all clamber back on the bus and we'd sing all the way home. We were only ten or eleven years old, but that was the norm at the time. There's no way parents would allow that these days, but it was the age of innocence then, when nobody believed that anything bad could happen.

I still vividly remember the time we were taken to the Gaeltacht from Athlone. I must have been about eleven. Like everyone else who goes to the Gaeltacht, we were warned, 'When you get to Galway, if you're heard speaking English, you're off home again.' I'd only got off the train, of course, and I spoke English. The Brother put me back on the train and they rang Ma to say I was on my way home.

Ma waited for me in Athlone and put me straight back on the next Galway train, with a note to the Brother: *I paid £14 for the two weeks, don't send him home again.* So I went from Athlone to Galway, back to Athlone and back to Galway again in one afternoon, like a parcel. In fact, that sums up my schooldays: I wasn't 'bold', I didn't misbehave – not deliberately, anyway – and I kept my nose clean, but I was a natural clown and once I'd got a taste for it, there was no stopping me. School for me was a social thing, absolutely not an academic exercise.

FIVE

Mad World

In 1971 my mother was diagnosed with breast cancer and for a time I went completely off the rails. We were living in Athlone at the time, having moved there the year before, but she had to go to hospital in Dublin for an operation to remove her left breast. Up until then she had never even gone for a night out with my father since we were born. She used to say, 'I've no interest in crossing the door at night until the children are older.' She felt it was important that she was there in the evenings when we came in from playing and that she was there when we went to bed.

As you can imagine, the three of us, who'd had our mother by our sides every moment of our lives until then, were devastated. I wasn't even twelve at that point, Gerard was only nine and a half and Maeve just five. Gerard took it badly, but he went into himself, internalising his distress. In contrast, I caused mayhem, getting into fights with other kids at school and giving cheek. I can remember some of the Marist Brothers trying to talk to me about it, asking me how my mother was and how I was coping. My answer? 'You mind your own business.'

It wasn't that I didn't care – inside, I was terribly frightened, and this came out as anger, throwing my coat on the ground when I came in from school – Ma would have killed me if she could see me – and going into tantrums. I also started shoplifting at that time, thinking, 'Ma isn't here to stop me, so why not?' I was terrified: a cancer diagnosis in 1971 could mean death and I was scared that I'd lose my mother.

You'd think that visiting her would improve matters, but it actually made things worse, at least for me. Ma would be in bed, looking frail, and then we'd have to leave her and go home to an empty house, with all those feelings of fear stirred up again.

All the neighbours took turns to mind us, and looking back, it was brilliant the way the community in Athlone came together for us, even though we'd only been living there for a year. Of course, I hated it. I wasn't in my mother's house, wasn't eating my mother's food, but I had to put on a brave face. I remember thinking that it was all Athlone's fault: I'd had a perfect childhood in Ballyfermot and then we had to leave and I reasoned that if we'd stayed where we were, she wouldn't have got sick. Silly, of course, but I wasn't exactly feeling logical.

Maeve was too young for the neighbourhood rota, so Dad took her to work with him. He'd park in front of the window of whatever union meeting he was attending so that he could see her in the car, waiting for him. Can you imagine? He took us out of school to Eileen's for Ma's operation, I remember, so we'd be close at hand. Eileen woke us up one morning and said, 'Right, get up and we'll say a decade of the rosary. Your mum's going to have her operation in ten minutes' time.' It wasn't exactly tactful, but it gave us something to do while we were waiting to hear news.

In the end, Ma's operation went well and she came back home after a few weeks. Her illness was never really spoken about and she threw herself back into her role of mam again, cooking, shopping and cleaning. She never properly looked back or gave herself time to come to terms with things. My mother never smoked or drank and her cancer came as a shock to all of us, but particularly to my father, who was a heavy smoker. She lived a healthy lifestyle, while he lived an unhealthy one, and yet she got the cancer.

A few weeks after my mother came home from hospital my father took her to the pictures. He had a cigarette on the way from the car to the cinema and at the door of the Ritz he crumpled up his box of twenty Sweet Afton and told my mother he was never smoking again. And he never did. He went from years of smoking up to eighty cigarettes a day to going cold turkey. Now, that would have been hard, because in the 1970s there were no restrictions on smoking. And often my mother would get so fed up with his grouchy humour that she'd beg him to start again, but he never did.

My childhood smoking turned into a fifty-year habit, and it took me hundreds of thousands of cigarettes to finally kick the habit, but with the money Dad saved from not smoking any more, my parents were able to go on foreign holidays every year. They went all over Europe, to Russia, and, when my father found religion after his two heart attacks, which I'll go into later, the Holy Land. So many people say that they have a new lease of life after cancer, if they are lucky enough to survive, and Ma made the most of it.

Later, my mother told me that when she was in hospital waiting to have her operation, she was apprehensive about the operation and worried about all of us, so she sat down on a hospital chair and allowed herself a little cry. An old nun walked by. (Hospitals at this time were run by religious orders.) My mother later described the nun as 'a great big lump of a thing'. The nun stopped and said sternly, 'What's wrong with you?'

My mother, expecting a kind word and a bit of sympathy, said, 'Sister, I've got cancer and I'm going to die.'

The nun folded her arms, and, looking angrily at my mother, said, 'Get down on your two knees this minute and pray to God for forgiveness.' My mother's mouth fell open in shock. 'Only God knows if and when you are going to die,' the nun continued, 'not the doctors, and certainly not you. Now, pray for forgiveness for second-guessing God and after you do that, we don't want to hear any more talk about dying.'

When my mother told me that story, years later, I said, 'I hope you gave her what for.'

She thought for a moment and said, 'It was exactly what I needed at that moment. I was worrying about dying when I should have been thinking about getting better. The nun was right.'

When she did get home to Athlone after her operation, a girl who lived on our road knocked at the door and said that a nun in the Bower Convent School wanted to see my mother at her earliest convenience. Ma couldn't understand why – my sister didn't even go to that school – but she thought it might be important, so the next day she went to the school and asked to see the nun. A little wizened old nun came out and beckoned her into a room close by.

'Hello, Sister, I'm Esther Cowan. I believe you want to see me.'

The little old nun patted my mother on the arm, gave her a big smile and said, 'I had the very same operation thirty years ago. You'll be fine.' And with that, she walked out of the room, leaving my mother standing there with her mouth hanging open. The nun grapevine had clearly been in action!

My mother thought that what that old nun did was fabulous. It cheered her up no end. It was the first time she had met a breast-cancer survivor. Oh, she'd been given all the figures and percentages about the recovery success stories, but she'd not met anyone who'd had a breast removed because of cancer. And those two sentences lifted my mother's spirits more than anything had done since she had been diagnosed.

My mother was told that she'd have to go back to the doctor who had operated on her, Bob O'Connell, every six months for five years and then once a year after that for another five years. On her first visit, she was told that everything looked good, all the cancer had been removed and it hadn't come back. So it was all good news.

'Have you any questions?' the doctor asked, after he did his examination.

'Just one,' my mother replied. 'People are asking if I've been sent for physiotherapy. What is it and do I need it?'

The doctor thought for a moment and said, 'Can you lift your arm up in the air?' He demonstrated what he meant by lifting his own arm up, as if he were trying to reach the ceiling.

'I can,' said my mother, doing the same thing.

'Well, that's all the physiotherapy you need,' said Dr O'Connell. 'I'll see you back here in six months.'

My mother was still unsure. 'But ...' she began.

'Mrs Cowan,' the doctor interrupted. 'You're not an invalid, so don't make an invalid out of yourself.'

This might see patronising nowadays, but these words of advice were words my mother heeded. She thought that what the doctor and the nuns had said to her encouraged her to get better. These days if a nun spoke to a cancer patient like 'the big lump of a thing' had spoken to my mother, the woman would be on to Joe Duffy's *Liveline* radio show to complain. Back in the seventies, if you got ill, you were encouraged to try to get better, and if a harsh word was needed, that's what you got. In my mother's case, it worked.

A decade later, Dad would get the first of two heart attacks and he dealt with them very differently. Not having been a Catholic, or a bit interested in religion, he suddenly found God and, in particular, the Russian Orthodox Church. Looking back, it probably wasn't that surprising as he had a strong interest in Russia, being a trade unionist, but his faith certainly brought him attention in suburban Dublin in the eighties.

Da's two heart attacks frightened the life out of him, but we weren't quite as devastated as we'd been when Ma had got ill. It wasn't that we didn't care, it was just that he wasn't the centre of the home in the way she was; and because we were teenagers by then, we were more independent. However, my mother was lost without Da. He always gave her his wage packet – every last cent of it, except for his cigarette money. Ma looked after the housekeeping, but he'd pay the bills and later, when he died, she didn't know how to pay a bill.

Dad had his first heart attack when I was a teenager and his second in the 1980s. I was working in EMI at the time, and had a car, which I only got in 1984, and used to drive Ma down to St Vincent's Hospital to see him. He recovered, but I remember him coming out of hospital and announcing, 'I'm converting to the Russian Orthodox Church.' I think he was looking for something spiritual, but Judaism or Islam wouldn't have interested him.

'But you're a Catholic,' Ma insisted, even though she knew he wasn't a Mass-goer. They were a very close couple; they did everything together, and they loved a good political conversation – Ma hated Fianna Fáil but, with typical perversity, loved Charlie Haughey! However, religion was something they rarely discussed. We didn't much care; we figured that it was his business.

Ma's faith was deep and very important to her and Dad respected that. She and Eileen had this unwavering faith, which had helped them through Ma's cancer, but outside of the chapel they didn't like to be preached to, which reminds me of a couple of funny stories. I can still remember Miriam, the sister of one of Ma's friends, a born-again Christian who'd talk about God to anyone who'd listen. Miriam called in to visit one evening after tea when my mother was knitting another of our jumpers and while she was trying to share God's love with Esther, Ma just put her knitting down and folding her hands over her ball of wool, smiled in a superior way and said, 'I don't need to be born again, Miriam. I got it right the first time.'

Many years later, when Ma was a lot older and going to her club for the elderly, there was a debate doing the rounds about whether priests should be allowed to marry. One of the other old ladies, who was always complaining about the rules of the church, asked one day, 'Esther, do you think priests should be allowed to marry?'

Quick as a flash, Ma replied, 'I suppose so … if they love each other.'

I don't know where she got me because I never had her faith. I think I wanted to when I was very young, but I just never felt in a state of grace anywhere in the Catholic Church. When I was making my first Communion I thought that once I did that I would feel Jesus in my life, but sadly no. I felt no different. When I was seventeen, I took a holiday in Rome and I wondered if I'd feel holy there, but while the opulence, grandeur and priceless works of art on show just stunned me, none of it made me feel holy. The only place where I ever felt in a state of grace was at the Western Wall in Jerusalem. To look at it, it's just a very old wall, but due to Temple Mount entry restrictions for Jews, the Western Wall is the holiest place where they are allowed to pray and it's the only place in the world where I feel extremely close to God.

Whatever his reasoning, my dad had made his choice, but at the time, there was no Russian Orthodox church in Ireland, so occasionally we'd get visits from Father Alexis from London. He wore a big black hat and billowing black robes, and when he visited, he'd sing grace before meals, in Russian. I'd say the neighbours would have been fascinated, hearing that coming through the walls!

I was living away at the time in flats and bedsits and Maeve was away in college studying to be a teacher; only Gerard was still living at home, so there was always room, and Ma would make up beds for Father Alexis and the younger priest who often accompanied him. She looked after them well, and she fed them, and now and then she'd say to Da, 'Come on, we'll all go out for a trip to Glendalough,' which they would, the priests in their full regalia!

Sometimes Father Alexis and the other priest would go for walks around the neighbourhood and Ma would say, 'Sweet Jesus, what will the neighbours think, and them all in black, with their long beards: they're the image of Rasputin.' She'd peer through the curtains as they headed off down the road, mortified, but as soon as they came back, she'd be all smiles. 'Ah, did you have a nice walk?' She never got used to those Russian Orthodox priests coming to the house.

Years later, when the Orthodox church here was established and had its own priests, two of them called up to see my father when he was dying. At this time, we were living in Balally, just up the hill from Dundrum, and we had two 'good rooms', one in the front and one in the back, with a door between them. One Sunday evening I dropped around and Da was in the front room with the priests, who had called in to see how he was, because he was too ill to go to church.

Ma was be in the back room. 'Now look at them,' she said, at the top of her voice, nodding in their direction. 'Calling up at teatime. They knew I'd be cooking for somebody – but they're getting nothing.' Looking back, I have a feeling that she may have been experiencing the early onset of her dementia, but at the time, her behaviour just seemed a bit rude.

'Ma, they might be able to hear you,' I said.

'I don't care if they can hear me. Who calls into somebody's house at six in the evening? They can smell the cooking,

90

that's what it is. These churches are all the same, they all just want money.' Of course, she couldn't not offer them something, so she went into the front room, muttering, 'They wouldn't turn up at eleven o'clock in the morning, would they?'

She offered them something to eat, saying sweetly, 'Will you have a bite to eat, Fathers?'

'Oh, no thanks, Mrs Cowan. We've already eaten,' the older man said.

Ma came back in to me. 'Now, what do you think of that? They won't even eat the food I'm offering them – they won't be coming back here again! I've never been so insulted.' I desperately tried to hold in the laughter, while, being the good hostess, she had to go back into them: 'Would you like a cup of tea?'

'Oh, thank you, Mrs Cowan,' the older man said. 'I'll have a lemon tea.'

'What?' Ma said. 'Is that Lyons's?'

'No, just a cup of tea with no milk and sugar, just a slice of lemon.'

In she came to me in the back room. 'Do you hear that? They want lemon tea! Thank God I have a lemon.' She went into the kitchen and cut a lemon into four wedges, sticking a wedge in each cup of tea, and as she had one left over, she put it in her own cup. 'I'm going to try this lemon tea

myself.' She took a sip. 'Oh, my Jesus, I couldn't drink that. How do they drink that? They're not normal people,' she said at the top of her voice. My poor mother – what she had to put up with!

SIX

Cum on Feel the Noize

Meeting Justin Rooney was a turning point in my young life, but before I tell you how and when it happened, you need to know this about gay people. they can spot other gay people and know they are gay. It's true. You can be at the supermarket, the record shop, in school, or walking down a crowded street. Even in a venue with three thousand people, a gay guy can spot another gay guy. Now, I didn't know I was gay at the time. I knew that I was different, but I couldn't quite put my finger on what it was – until I met Justin.

I can be precise about the day we met. It was 24 March 1973. I was thirteen years of age. Slade were on stage in the National Stadium, Dublin, and Noddy Holder was belting out 'Cum on feel the Noize'. Slade were the loudest band I had ever heard. I'd seen Thin Lizzy and Hawkwind when I was living in Limerick and the Slade concert was my third gig. Now that I think of it, my parents had probably allowed me to go because I'd been sent on my own the previous year to see my cousins in London. This was a big deal for my family, with our republican heritage, but as usual, Ma had seen the bigger picture. After the bloodbath of Bloody Sunday in January of that year, tensions North and South were high, with protests and the burning of the British Embassy in Dublin. The talk everywhere, including in the school yard, was of Bloody Sunday, and from memory it seems that we were all of one mind: when we were older we were going to join the IRA and fight the Brits and avenge the deaths of the thirteen people killed in Derry. And for the next few months this was all that we talked about. We went to see Bernadette Devlin, a civil rights leader and MP from Derry, giving a speech in Shannon. We listened to older lads telling us why we should join the IRA. Bloody Sunday was everywhere and for a while I got caught up in the frenzy of it. Britain, and the British, were the enemy and there was nobody to tell us not to get involved.

In sending me to London, Ma quashed my own little rebellion, even if I was determined I wasn't going to enjoy two weeks in a city full of enemies. So what happened? I loved every minute of it, that's what happened. That holiday started my love affair with London. My cousins took me to Oxford Street and to all the sights. My uncle Johnny took me to the Tower of London. I was a big Tudor fan and to see the spot where Anne Boleyn was beheaded was riveting to me. However, Johnny also told me a story that for years afterwards, I thought was true. He told me, in all seriousness, that Anne Boleyn was from West Ham and Henry VIII had founded the West Ham football club so he could see a match on a Saturday afternoon when he was spending the weekend with Anne before they got married. His wife at the time, Catherine of Aragon, was a jealous woman, so he set up the club, so he could say he was having a sporty few days away with the lads, and to keep the Queen's eye off the real reason he was going away every weekend. How I ever managed to do well afterwards in history exams I'll never know.

Back in the National Stadium, I couldn't believe the reaction of the audience to this show. The girls' screams and the boys' roars sounded like a jet starting up. Like everyone else there, I was singing along, waving my arms in the air, swaying to the music and having a great time.

Suddenly something slammed into the side of my head, sending me reeling. A wave of nausea washed over me as I dropped to my knees. It was all I could do not to throw up or pass out. 'You're from St Benildus, aren't you?' a voice shouted over the noise of the band, referring to the secondary school in Stillorgan that I'd started attending the previous year. I looked up to see a tall skinny guy in loon pants, a T. Rex T-shirt and shoulder-length wavy hair, holding a wooden seat, the seat he had just clobbered me with.

'Yeah,' I replied, putting both arms over my head to block the next assault.

'Get up, you dozy mare,' he said, in mock annoyance, 'I'm not going to hit you again. If I'd recognised you from behind, I wouldn't have walloped you in the first place. C'mon, let's get out of here, it's bleedin' mental.' He glanced around with a look of disgust on his face. 'I'm more of a Roxy Music fan myself. Slade attracts a very rough element,' he added without a hint of irony.

'Well, you'd be that rough element,' I angrily muttered, as he dropped the chair, took hold of my hand and helped me to my feet. 'What the fuck are you playing at and who are you?' Needless to say, I was seriously pissed off and shook his helping hand away.

'I'm Justin and I was a year ahead of you at school, but I left,' he said matter-of-factly, not even noticing I was angry. 'I'm a trainee hair stylist now. I've always been good with hair, you know. I could do something with yours, if you like. C'mon, let's get out of here. We're going to be great friends.'

He took hold of my hand again and led me out of the stadium. It took about ten minutes to get through the heaving crowd, who all seemed hell-bent on launching themselves at the stage. As we were leaving the show, hand in hand, I got the feeling that my life was going to change that night. Who *is* this guy and why am I holding his hand in public? I thought, as a rush of excitement swept over me.

We went out of the stadium and into a grim night; the sky was overcast and a wind blew up the South Circular Road that'd cut through you, and all I was wearing was a frayed pair of jeans and a thin cotton Slade T-shirt. I didn't mind, though. I was looking forward to getting to know Justin better on our walk into town. There was something about him that intrigued me.

'I'm glad to be out of that kip,' he said, running his fingers through his hair, which was damp with sweat, and trying to fluff it up. 'I'm sweatin' like a pig here. It's not a good look for a white woman,' he said dramatically, causing me to snigger. 'Fighting's not usually my style,' he added, fanning his face with his right hand, 'but flinging seats around and causing mayhem is what it's all about, isn't it? Better than being a smelly hippy looking for peace and love. I'm really sorry if I hurt you, by the way,' he said apologetically. 'Let's go to Bartley Dunne's and you can tell me all about yourself. What's your name?'

'Rory,' I answered, wondering if going to a pub at my age with a complete stranger was a good idea. I hadn't heard of Bartley Dunne's, but it was an iconic Dublin pub at the time, home to actors, couples, students and, as it turned out, gay men. Homosexuality was a crime until 1993, so discretion was the name of the game and Bartley Dunne's was one of a handful of pubs where the gay community could meet.

'Okay, Rory, and what name do you want to go by in Bartley's?'

'Rory. That's my name.' I had no idea what he was talking about.

'No, you dizzy cow. Are you sure I didn't rattle your brains when I hit you with that chair? Look, you have to pick a different name on the scene. You don't want to be blackmailed, do you? If you use your real name, you could be,' he said casually, as if this was the norm. 'They could tell your ma you're a queer,' he continued, in case I hadn't understood him. 'You don't want your ma to know you're a queer, do you? So you pick a different name, like Dorian or something. That way, if someone says to your ma that her son Dorian is bent, she'll say she doesn't have a son called Dorian. And she'll never suspect it's you the blackmailer is talking about.'

I couldn't believe what I was hearing. He was like a whirlwind. How did he know I was gay?

'How do you know I'm queer?' I muttered.

'Oh, I can spot them,' he said, tapping his nose twice, indicating that this gift he had was a secret. Did he think ignorance was bliss as far as I was concerned? To hell with that. I wanted to know the signs that showed him I was gay, because if he could see them, then surely other people could too, and that could lead to a lot of trouble.

'But what is it about me that you can spot?' The panic was rising in my voice. I was imagining schoolmates, queer-bashers, teachers and the guards recognising I was gay, and the anxiety of it all hit me in the pit of my stomach.

'Your hair, your clothes, your mannerisms, the way you stand, how you act, the aftershave you wear,' he rattled off. 'All the signs are there.'

I stopped walking and stared at him. 'Ah, you've got to be joking.' Was I that strange that anyone at all would notice? I thought about my parents and brother and sister and wondered if it was written in neon above my head.

'I'm not joking,' he replied, 'but don't worry. Only another Nellie would see the signs. Nobody else will cop it. Now, what name do you want to go by on the scene?'

'Well, I like the name Andy,' I answered, not sure what he meant by 'the scene'.

'Okay, that's settled. You're Andy on the scene and I'm Philip. So, don't forget, we don't use our real names. Now, you let me be your fairy godmother and I'll show you the ropes.'

So that was that. I was Andy and Justin was Philip. I felt excited about having a new name. As Andy, I could have a new past life too, not like the boring one I'd had until now. The idea of reinventing my past and becoming someone new was so 'now': Mark Feld had reinvented himself as Marc Bolan; David Jones had become David Bowie and then Ziggy Stardust. This is going to be fantastic, I thought.

'Oh yeah, one other thing. Because my trade name is Philip, I'm also known as Phyllis,' Justin said, interrupting my thoughts. 'We'll have to think up a girl's name for you. I don't see the possibilities with female versions of Rory or Andy, but don't worry, your auntie Phyllis will come up with something.' And with this, his hands in his jeans pockets and his head down against the wind, Justin walked ahead and didn't notice I'd stopped dead in my tracks.

'What sort of a place are you bringing me to?' I said, getting a little bit worried about what I was letting myself in for. 'And why do I have to have a girl's name?'

'Bartley Dunne's,' he said, exasperated. 'And you have a girl's name because it's part of the gay armour. Let's say I ring you at home some night. Well, your ma and your da could be listening to what you're saying. So you say something like, "Howya, Phyllis, I was out last night with Marsha and Connie." Your ma and da think you're taking to a girl and you were out with girls the night before, when in fact you're talking about fellas.'

It all made some sort of sense, even if it seemed a bit weird. But the part about parents listening in to phone calls had the ring of truth about it. My mother had great hearing. If I ever got up in the middle of the night to go downstairs for a cigarette – and blow the smoke up the chimney so she wouldn't smell it the next day – she would hear me the minute I'd tippy-toe out of my bedroom.

'Who's that?' she'd roar from her bedroom.

'It's me. Go back to sleep,' I'd reply in a hushed tone. I didn't want the whole house up: I just wanted a sneaky cigarette. I'd have been gasping for one all evening but had to wait until the rest of the family had gone to bed. Ma would have killed me if she knew that I smoked.

'What are you doing up at this hour of the night?'

At this point, I'd be exasperated. All I'd want was a quiet smoke and there'd be all this palaver. 'I'm just going downstairs to get a glass of water,' I'd reply, in what I hoped was a cheery voice.

'Will you bring me up one too?' she'd bellow. I'd never get to have my sneaky cigarette. It just wouldn't seem worth the hassle. So I understood exactly what Justin was talking about when he said Ma and Da could be listening to my phone conversations. They would be and they did, even if they didn't need to know the details. My mother didn't want to know what my phone conversations were about; she just wanted to get the gist of what I was talking about to make sure 'You aren't getting up to any shenanigans.' By this, she meant the kind of thing that might bring me to the attention of the guards – something that seemed to happen more often after meeting Justin, even if it was the kind of harmless mischief that came with boredom. At that time, we were all bored – it seemed to go with the territory of being a teenager. But now, life looked as if it would become a whole lot more interesting.

'And who are Marsha and Connie?' I asked.

'I'll introduce you when we get to the pub. Marsha is a fella called Joe. He's from Mallow in County Cork. Marsha Mallow, get it? And Connie is Colin. He races pigeons. He doesn't race them himself, if you know what I mean. His pigeons race other pigeons. He just owns a few. Connie's as butch as nails. She's built like a brick shithouse, with a face like Desperate Dan and an Adam's apple like a Rooster potato. He likes dressing up in women's clothes. Not in the pubs, but at house parties. He's a nice aul queen. You'll like them all. You'll see. Now, do you want a bit of eyeliner to show off those big blue eyes? And if the barman asks, tell him you're eighteen.'

I didn't know what type of a place Justin was bringing me to, or what kind of people he was going to introduce me to, but I did know my life was never going to be the same again.

We got to Bartley Dunne's and went in. I don't know what I was expecting, but this wasn't it. To my relief, the pub wasn't full of perverts molesting other people. It was a pub with normal, everyday people having a drink and a chat. So what happened to us? We got barred, that's what. It turns out that gay bars don't want garda attention. The bar could be closed down in an instant if it was serving underage drinkers. Justin was all right; he was nearly fifteen and if the gardaí raided the bar he could just grab a bar towel and start cleaning a table and make it look like he was working there as a lounge boy. (At fourteen years of age in 1974 you could work in a pub as a lounge boy or girl, but you couldn't drink alcohol in a pub until you were eighteen.) But I was only thirteen. If I was caught in there, the pub owner would be charged and could lose his licence and the customers could probably have their names taken and published in the *Evening Herald* for being in a known gay establishment with an underage boy in it. It wasn't in anybody's interest for me to be in Bartley Dunne's that night.

When we went in, a customer was chatting to the barman and I could see him inclining his thumb towards me. 'They're looking a bit young these days, aren't they?' I heard him saying.

The barman turned to Justin and shouted 'You! Out!' and, pointing at me, added 'Go home and do your homework.'

I was mortified. I could feel my face going crimson. I didn't know where to look. Everyone in the bar was staring at me. I stood there glued to the spot. I couldn't move. This seemed to annoy the barman, a surly bastard if ever there was one. He came rushing out from behind the bar and with a wave of his hands shouted, 'Out, I said, out now! You're barred!'

I just wanted to leave as quickly as possible. But Justin wasn't going to go quietly, even though he wasn't being barred. 'Shove your pub up your hole,' he shouted over his shoulder. 'I don't want to drink in a dump with a narky old bollocks like you behind the bar anyway.'

It would be another few weeks – and an attempt to make myself look older, so I could pass for an eighteen-year-old – before I went back to Bartley Dunne's.

And that's how I met Justin, or Philip, or Phyllis.

SEVEN

No More Mr
Nice Guy

The 1970s were fantastic in many ways – the music and fashion and attitudes – but I also remember being bored a lot of the time. That might not have been such a bad thing in itself, but put boredom, me and Justin Rooney together and trouble was never far behind. Justin was a kindred spirit, the two of us young gay men trying to find a place for ourselves in the world. And he was always up for a laugh. Really, that was the whole basis of our friendship, having a laugh and getting into mischief together. It was never any deeper than that – we'd never talk about feelings or emotions.

Looking back, there were signs right from the beginning that all wasn't well with Justin, but I was young and I didn't see anything wrong with his mood swings. I can remember one night when he'd been unusually down.

'This is a kip,' he'd said, gesturing to the city around us. 'When I'm eighteen, I'm moving to London.' This kind of outburst would become more and more common as we got older. Back then, I didn't understand. Instead, I suggested that we play another prank for a laugh. But he didn't bite. 'Nah, let's go home,' he said, with a tiny hint of despair in his voice. 'I'll see you tomorrow.' He lit another cigarette and slowly walked away, his head down, like he had the weight of the world on his shoulders. I walked the opposite way towards my house, trying to shake off the feeling of foreboding that had hit me. This was beyond my understanding at the time.

For me, Justin represented the freedom to be myself. I was very good at compartmentalising things and Justin fitted into the box marked 'gay'. I didn't want any of my school friends to know that I was gay, for obvious reasons, but with Justin, I could be me. When I was doing my Inter Cert, now the Junior Cycle, Ma sent me to the Institute of Education on Leeson Street for grinds and supervised study – for all the good it did me! I'd shove my schoolbag in a hedge and head off into town to Bartley Dunne's, now that I was old enough to look the part.

The next day, though, it was business as usual. Tapping phones gave us endless hours of amusement. We'd go into a public phone box and by dialling the numbers one, nine and zero and then tapping all the other numbers out by pressing rapidly on the buttons, we'd get through to our target and we didn't have to pay for the call. We'd pick a public phone box on the main Sandyford Road, just around the corner from where I lived. I'd go through the phone book trying to find people with strange names. We could have fun with those.

Justin loved doing ad lib performances on the phone. He got into whatever role he was playing and he wouldn't give up until he drove the person on the other end of the line mad. And if they hung up before they lost the plot and started shouting back at him, he'd ring them back.

One night at about 12.30 a.m., he called this unsuspecting woman.

'Hello?' she said anxiously.

In the seventies, you wouldn't think of ringing anybody after 10 p.m., unless it was an emergency. A call at that hour of the night usually meant bad news. The poor woman probably thought someone belonging to her had died.

'Howya, Missus!' shouted Justin in his best Tipperary accent. 'A friend of mine lives next door to you. Would you mind going in to wake up the aul bollocks and tell him I want to talk to him on the phone. Would you do that, Missus, like a good woman?'

I had my cravat stuffed in my mouth trying to muffle my snorts of laughter. (Yes, I really did wear a cravat!)

'Jesus, Mary and Joseph,' the woman screamed. 'You nearly gave me a heart attack ringing at this hour of the night. Do you know what time it is?' We did indeed know what time it was, but we were having far too much fun.

Justin was really getting into his role now. 'Listen you,' the woman screeched down the phone line, 'the only thing I'm going to do is hang up and ring the police. I'm certainly not going next door to wake Mr O'Connell up.'

Justin immediately roared back, 'O'Connell? And, acting perplexed, he added, 'Is that 956437?' Laughing, he hung up.

But our luck ran out when we decided to phone Mr Cecil Dick, a name I had discovered when browsing the phone book for our next victim.

'Oh, fabulous,' Justin said, a big grin on his face. 'Can I do this one? I'll be better at it than you. Where's the phone number?' I tapped the number and when a woman at the other end answered, Justin became this camp queen with a slow drawl: 'Helloooo. Could I speak to Cesssssil Dick, pleasssse? It's Phylisssss here. 'He drew his S's out and he sounded like Kaa the snake from *The Jungle Book* singing, 'Trust In Me'.

He was just about to say something else when he saw a garda and a ban garda (as women gardaí were still called at the time) walking towards us. They were only a couple of yards away. Justin hastily hung up and, in our panic, we stumbled out of the phone box. We must have looked as guilty as sin.

'What are you two up to?' the ban garda asked. She was a large woman: a phrase I'd heard my mother use, 'Beef to the heels, like a Mullingar heifer,' would have been a very accurate description.

'Nothing,' I replied sheepishly. 'We were just ringing the operator to get a phone number.'

'Is that right?' large ban garda asked. 'You were tapping the phone, you pair of gurriers, weren't you?'

'We certainly were not,' Justin protested.

'Don't tell lies, you pair of nancy boys,' she said disdainfully. 'We saw you. I've a mind to arrest the pair of you.'

Just then my mother walked out of the laneway beside the phone box. My face fell when I saw her. She stared at the two gardaí interrogating myself and Justin and she gave me a look I knew well. It said, 'Just you wait till I get you home.'

'Rory!' she snapped. 'What's going on?'

The ban garda, bristling with self-importance, asked, 'And who are you?'

Esther looked her up and down and said scornfully, 'I'm his mother and I'd like to know what your business is with him.'

'We think your son and his *friend* were tapping the phone,' the ban garda said, emphasising the word 'friend' to make it sound dirty.

I could feel myself flushing. 'We weren't, Ma,' I said, lying through my teeth. My heart was thumping.

'You heard him. He. Said. He. Didn't. Do. It,' she said, emphasising every word, 'so he didn't do it. And if all you've got is that you think he was tapping the phone, whatever that is, then I'm taking my son and his friend with me. And when you know for certain, and not just *think* you know, then come back to us. Until then, I'd advise you to stop harassing minors.'

But the ban garda wasn't willing to let it go. 'Your son's very effeminate,' she sniffed.

My mother gave her a withering look and replied, 'Compared to you, I suppose he is.' And with that, the three of us walked away, leaving a crimson-faced ban garda and her partner, who had said nothing at all through all this, trying to stifle a laugh.

'Thanks, Ma,' I said appreciatively. 'I don't know what we would have done if you hadn't come. We did nothing, I swear.'

She was looking at me as if to say, Do you take me for a fool? But then I came up with the clincher: 'You were great dealing with that policewoman. I'm really proud that you're my ma.'

That did it. I could see her mouth turning up, her shoulders went back and she walked taller, and I'm nearly sure there was a tiny tear in her eye.

Of course, my mother probably 'knew' that I was gay, but there's knowing and knowing, and while she must have been aware that I was different, the subject never came up for discussion, not for many years anyway. But I knew that my mother would always be in my corner. This might well be why I never felt confusion or shame about who I was, because she and Da accepted me. Quite honestly, I don't think it would have occurred to Da that I might be gay; I don't think that he could conceive of such a thing; he was just from that generation where men were men and women were women. But he was never less than supportive.

I wasn't a real troublemaker as a teenager and most of what I got up to with Justin was the product of boredom, as it was for so many of us then, with very little to entertain us, and even though Ma would often tell me that she didn't know how she'd ended up with a boy like me, she seemed to find the humour in our antics – most of the time. Even when we gatecrashed Mass in a wheelchair ...

Sunday was a dreary day in the mid-1970s and would have loved a lie-in on Sunday mornings, but my mother would always get me up and out for nine o'clock Mass every Sunday. It would start at 8 a.m. with, 'Rory, are you up yet?' shouted from the kitchen.

I'd grunt and turn over in bed.

A few minutes later: 'Rory, I won't call you again! There's a cup of tea here for you. It'll go cold if you don't get down here *now*! And don't you dare think about eating anything, or you won't be able to take Communion. Now get up and get down to Mass.'

At this point, she knew that I didn't actually go into the church, but she still wouldn't let me stay in bed. 'I can only send you out to Mass, I can't force you to go,' she'd say, infuriated. 'But don't expect me to play a part in you missing Mass, you heathen. You can get out of this house in time for nine o'clock Mass and don't come back here until it's over.'

With that she'd slap down the Sunday newspaper on the kitchen table to indicate that the matter was closed. End of conversation.

So that's how Justin and I ended up walking around Dundrum on a dreary Sunday morning, looking for something to do. I'd called in to him on the way down to the village, hoping that he'd be up. 'We'll find something to do,' he said hopefully. But there was never anything to do at that hour on a Sunday morning. None of the shops, apart from the newsagent's, was open. When we were bored, we tended to get into mischief. It was always that way when Justin and I got together.

'You stay away from Justin Rooney,' my mother would warn me. 'I've heard all about him. He'll lead you into trouble.' Did I ever heed my mother's advice? Not even for a moment!

Now, we'd spotted an empty wheelchair parked on the path in the middle of Dundrum hill. 'Maybe whoever owned it died and the family don't want it lying around the house reminding them of their dead granny or granddad, so they dumped it,' said Justin. There was a pause before he said enthusiastically: 'C'mon, let's take it – for a laugh.'

'What are we going to do with it, just push each other around in it?' I asked in my bored voice.

'No,' said Justin eagerly, 'let's take it up to my house. I'll borrow my granny's fur coat and hat and scarf and I've a wig I robbed from work. I'll put them on and you can push me down to twelve o'clock Mass. We can pretend I'm your granny and we'll have a laugh.' He was delighted with the idea. 'If anyone asks, just tell them we live miles away. Tell them we can't afford the bus fare and you're after pushing me all the way. Say you don't mind pushing me to Mass, because the walk to the church is downhill, but you're not looking forward to pushing me back home, because it's all uphill. I bet people will each give us fifty pence for the bus fare. It could be a nice little earner,' he said, arms wide open, hands turned up and a big grin on his face.

Of course, I joined in enthusiastically and we took off up Dundrum hill, taking turns to push each other in the wheelchair and feeling very excited. When we got to Justin's house, we could see the family through the front window, having breakfast and listening to the radio. We knew that Justin's parents and granny had been to eight o'clock Mass and wouldn't be going out for the rest of the day, so Granny wouldn't even notice that her Sunday clothes were missing. Justin sneaked in while I waited round the back. An upstairs window opened and a fur coat, hat and scarf came flying out, followed by a wig, a lipstick, a powder compact, a black dress, a pair of nylons and a bottle of Yardley's lavender perfume. As the items were being thrown out, I was running around the back garden gathering them all up and hurrying into the garden shed before I was seen.

In a couple of minutes, Justin joined me. 'Here, get that down your gob,' he announced, throwing me a sausage he'd taken off a plate in the kitchen. 'It's not the first time you heard that, you dirty tramp,' he said, squealing with laughter. I loved the bitchy banter we had going between us. No malice at all, though if anyone heard us, they'd assume we hated each other. I ate the sausage and we got to work dolling Justin up to look like an old woman. It was to be our first drag show.

When I had finished, I stood back to look at my handiwork. His make-up wasn't that badly done, if I do say so myself. 'You look fabulous,' I said. 'You could do drag. You could easily pass as a real old woman.'

'*Old* woman?' he screeched. Justin could be quite vain.

'Well no, not really,' I spluttered. 'You could pass as a ... princess.'

'It's better than looking like the Queen Mother. And that's who *you're* trying to make me look like. Still, it'll do the trick. C'mere,' he said, putting his hand to an imaginary pearl necklace, 'do you really think I could do drag? I could dress like a real Southern belle. Like Vivien Leigh in *Gone With the Wind*. I'd call myself Sarah Belle Palsy. You get it? Cerebral Palsy,' he added with a huge laugh.

'Oh, you're dreadful,' I replied in mock shock. 'That's not even funny.'

And with that we were off; him looking like the Queen Mother in the wheelchair and me pushing it. What seemed like a great idea at the time became less so the closer we got to the church.

Justin was in his element, however. 'Yoo-hoo!' he'd call out cheerily to random people.

'Don't make me laugh,' I warned. 'If I start laughing, I won't stop. My nerves are gone. Shot to bits they are. Look,' I said, holding out my hand to demonstrate how bad my anxiety was, 'I can't stop shaking.'

Adjusting his granny's fur hat and scarf, he said, 'Ah shut up, Baby Jane, and push the fuckin' wheelchair.' And with that, he went into his impersonation of Joan Crawford as Blanche in the film about the warring sisters, *Whatever Happened to Baby Jane?*, which was a favourite of ours. 'Jane,' he said dramatically, 'you wouldn't be able to do these awful things to me if I weren't in this chair.'

As Bette Davis in the role of Baby Jane, I replied, 'But you are, Blanche! You are in that chair!'

When we got to the church, I had the feeling that things were not going to go as planned. I wheeled Justin up the aisle and he started grabbing people's arms, raising his voice a couple of octaves in an attempt to sound like a woman, and pleading, 'Pray for me. The prognosis isn't good.' Or, 'Will you pray for me? My woman's problem is back,' pointing towards his groin. I thought he was taking things too far when he added, 'This is Rory from Balally Hill. He's my carer. He's looking really tired, isn't he? It's the cleaning jobs he does in the evenings that are wearing him out. But he has fines to pay,' he said, tut-tutting.

At this point, I was panicking. Now people knew my name and the road I lived on and they'd think I was a criminal. 'Blanche! Cut it out now!' I said, with more than a hint of despair.

'Rory, can we go up to the front? I want to go up to the altar,' Justin said hopefully. Oh, he was really enjoying himself. Without replying, I pushed the chair up towards the altar. Please, God, I said to myself, Don't let him do anything else. God, I promise I'll go to Mass every week if you'll just stop him embarrassing me any more.

Unfortunately, God must not have been listening, because as soon as the priest came out from the sacristy, Justin jumped out of the wheelchair and let out a roar: 'It's a miracle!' Then he did a little dance that put me in mind of the Beverly Hillbillies' Granny Clampett at a hootenanny, and ran out the side door of the church, leaving me with the empty wheelchair. I did what any other gay boy would do in a panicky situation: I lifted up my metaphorical skirts and legged it out the other side door.

I searched Dundrum high and low for Justin, but I couldn't find him anywhere. Just as well, I suppose, because I'd have torn strips off him. I ambled home, promising myself that I'd never speak to Justin Rooney ever again. He was brilliant fun, but he always took things that bit too far.

'How could you?' my mother shrieked as I came in through the front door. 'You wicked, blasphemous little liar. I've had phone calls from people telling me what you were up to in the chapel. With a wheelchair that was stolen from outside a care home! Mother of Jesus! If you go to court for this, you'll end up with your name in the paper and it'll be your own fault. And I'm sure all the neighbours know. And if they don't, they soon will. The news of what you did in the church will spread like wildfire,' she said bitterly.

My mother feared the twin evils of having her name in the paper and the neighbours knowing her business and I had ticked both off the list. I stood there resignedly, my head down, thinking that if the neighbours knew, it was probably as a result of her shouting and roaring.

'Well, have you anything to say for yourself?' she demanded, her voice rising again. 'Tell me exactly what happened, because when people stop me in the street – and they will, you mark my words,' she said, poking me in the chest. 'I want to know everything before they tell me. I don't want any nasty surprises. I need to be armed and able to cut them down to size.'

I decided to tell her the whole truth, from finding the wheelchair, getting the costume, make-up and wig, to Justin whizzing up the aisle asking people to pray for him. I could see her trying to swallow a giggle at that. And when I told her about Justin asking for prayers while pointing to his groin and saying his woman's trouble was back, she couldn't hold the laughter in any longer. She wiped the tears from her eyes and blurted, 'Get out of my sight. I'm sure I took the wrong baby home from the Coombe. Now go, I must ring our Eileen.'

As I was in the kitchen getting my breakfast, I could hear her on the phone to her sister: 'Eileen, you won't believe what he's done now.' There was a pause, but I couldn't hear what Eileen was saying. And then my mother replied, 'Eileen, you need to sit down for this one. This is a doozy! Rory,' she shouted, 'put the kettle on and bring me in a cup of tea.'

The next time I got up to mischief, it was entirely my own fault. I couldn't even blame Justin this time. It began when I wanted corkscrew curls, like Marc Bolan's. He was a big hero of mine and I loved his style, but my hair was dead straight with a centre parting and it hung halfway down my back. 'I can help you with that,' Justin said. I wasn't so sure about that. The last time Justin had 'helped' me with my hair, I thought my father was going to kill me, or at least disown me.

A few months previously, I'd decided I wanted blond highlights and with Justin working in a hairdresser's, I asked his advice. The fact that he was a trainee stylist and not a qualified hair expert didn't enter my mind at all.

'You can do it yourself at home,' he'd said confidently. 'It's very expensive to get highlights done in a salon. I'll get you the stuff you need. I'll just put everything in the hood of my duffel coat.'

This was a trick we used when we were shoplifting: one of us would wear a duffel coat and we'd walk around the supermarket looking at random items, while the other one walked casually past, dropping bars of chocolate or bags of sweets into the hood of the other person's coat. Then we'd walk out. Most times we weren't caught, but on the odd occasion we were, we used to feign complete innocence. 'I don't know how they got there,' we'd say. 'Someone must have dropped them into the hood for a joke.' Then the one of us who had put the chocolate or sweets in the other's hood would weigh in: 'Oh, I'd arrest him. I'd get the gardaí involved if I were you.' It always worked. The shop worker, or security guard, would laugh and think it was just one friend trying to embarrass the other. They'd take the stuff back, and off Justin and I would go. I should point out that shoplifting was a common thing in those days, when we didn't have a lot of spare cash for all the things we wanted. It was a rite of passage from childhood to adolescence and, even though it was wrong, we all did it.

Justin, true to his word, got the ingredients needed to put highlights in my hair. 'I'll come up to your house on Thursday afternoon. It's my day off and we'll do your *riah* then.'

'*Riah*' meant hair in Polari – hair spelled backwards. At this time on the gay scene, Polari was a language used by gay men so that others wouldn't understand what was being said. It was a real language and I think it originated in the theatre. *Naff* is Polari, in case you didn't know! Laurence Olivier was apparently fluent in Polari and Mr Pussy, an old friend of mine, could speak it. I know that Paul O'Grady knows a lot of it, even if it has died out now – there's no need for it any more. Anyway, in a crowded bar, one could say something like, '*Vada the dish on the ome with the palone*,' which means, 'Look at the arse on the young man with that woman.' A man saying that in English, at a time when homosexuality was illegal, risked being kicked to within an inch of his life.

Back to the highlights! When Thursday came, my mother was at work – she'd got a job in a make-up factory near where we lived. My father was still working as a union official in the ITGWU. My younger brother and sister were in school. I set out for school as normal that morning but sneaked back home when everyone else had left. I played records until about noon and then I went up for a bath. Justin was due at some time after twelve o'clock, so when I'd had my bath and washed my hair, I dried myself off and got ready for him to dye my hair.

Back in the seventies the only person in the family who had a dressing gown would be the mother. So, after I dried myself with a big old bath towel, I put on my mother's pink chenille dressing gown. Her pink fluffy slippers were lying there, so I slipped them on too, and went downstairs to wait for Justin to arrive.

Just after one o'clock, he turned up. 'Right, let's get going,' he said authoritatively, dropping a number of bags on the coffee table in the front room. 'This takes time. It's not what we stylists call "throwing a rinse through". Can you get me one of your ma's cereal bowls and I'll mix the colour. Now, where did I leave my foil strips?'. He rummaged through the bags. 'Oh, and while you're at it, bring me a towel so we don't get dye on your ma's dressing gown.'

When I gathered everything he'd asked for, I put on David Bowie's new album, *Station to Station*, brought a chair from the dining room and sat down. Justin snapped on a pair of rubber gloves. Holding his hands upright, he joked, 'Next patient, please.' Then he mixed up a colour with some bleach and some powder. When all the ingredients and all the tools he needed to do the job were in place, he started. 'I'll transform you. You'll look gorgeous!'

He did put on a good show. He must have been studying the stylists in the salon where he worked. He gathered up sections of my hair with the thin metal handle of a tail comb and arranged each on a foil strip. Then he slapped the dye mixture on with a spatula and folded the foil over the dyed patch of hair. After he'd done this a number of times, he stood back, sucking on the tail-comb handle. 'It's looking good so far. I'm brilliant with hair colour. You won't know yourself when I'm finished with you. Hang on a sec; I'll get that big ugly mirror you have hanging out in the hall and I'll show you what you look like.'

He came back with the long rectangular wall mirror in its brown wooden frame, handed it to me and said, 'Have a look.'

He was right. The hall mirror *was* ugly and old-fashioned, but my mother liked this type of stuff. The house was filled with old gas lamps, Toby jugs, Waterford Crystal vases, and a myriad of china ornaments that she had collected or inherited over the years. A few months earlier, a neighbour of ours, Elsie, who was living in her daughter's house, had come to visit. Her daughter and son-in-law were doing up their house and the builders were making a racket. Elsie couldn't take the noise any more and came over to see my mother. 'Oh, Mrs Cowan, the noise is driving me mad,' she'd moaned, blowing on her the cup of coffee. 'I suffer with migraines and the drilling has me climbing the walls.'

My mother had tut-tutted in sympathy and said, 'Call me Esther, please. You know, they're very lucky to have you, Elsie. Have another custard cream.'

'Oh, Esther, I just wish they'd stop all this decorating and hammering and drilling. Why can't they just have a house like yours, old-fashioned but nice?' And with that, she dunked her custard cream into her coffee.

I'd been in the kitchen listening to this exchange and I'd thought my mother would go apeshit. But she didn't. She just coughed and spluttered and, pretending she had something caught in her throat, she dashed out to the kitchen, where I found her hanging over the sink, tears of laughter running down her face. For years after that, right up until her dementia got bad, she always described her house as 'old-fashioned but nice'. And it was. Ma's ornaments, which were only knick-knacks to me, were precious to her, and there was a story behind every one. She remembered who'd left her what, which pieces were gifts, who had given them to her and which my father had bought for her.

After my father died, she asked me if there was anything I'd like left to me in her will. By this stage, I was in *Mrs Brown's Boys*, and I had everything I needed. 'Your house or whatever money you have is of no interest to me,' I said, and I could see sadness creeping into her eyes. 'Leave them to Gerard and Maeve,' I continued. 'But I'd love to have your ornaments.' Well, she jumped up from her chair with delight. Maybe old age is creeping up on me because ornaments that I once considered only dust collectors are now providing me with some very happy memories.

But back to Marc Bolan!

I put the mirror on the floor and gave my *riah* the once-over. I looked like something out of *Doctor Who* with all the silver foil in my hair, but I was impressed with Justin's work so far. I was getting excited. I wanted him to finish putting in the highlights and then there'd only be an hour's wait for the colour to take hold. 'Turn over the other side of the Bowie album before you start on the rest of the highlights,' I said, just as my father walked in the door. There was I, sitting on a kitchen chair with half my head covered in tinfoil strips, wrapped in my mother's pink dressing gown and wearing her pink fluffy slippers. Even today, I squirm when I remember it.

I'm dead, I thought. He's going to kill me. I wanted the ground to open up and swallow me.

'Oh, hello, Mr Cowan,' Justin said, greeting my father with a big grin and an exaggerated wave.

My father looked at Justin and then at me. Here it comes, I thought, he's going to explode. 'Are you going out tonight, son?' he asked, in his normal voice.

What's he playing at? I thought. 'I am, yeah,' I replied, my voice cracking with nervousness.

He took out his wallet and pulled out two one-pound notes and, handing them to me, he said, 'Well, enjoy yourself and make sure you don't get some girl into trouble.' I was stunned. I looked at my father, looked at the pink dressing gown and slippers I was wearing and looked into the mirror at my hair wrapped in tinfoil and thought to myself, he can't see what's in front of him. Justin started to laugh and muttered, 'The only way he's going to get a girl into trouble is if he tells her mother she's smoking.'

My father never did find out that I was gay, but Ma always knew, even if she never said anything directly. I was on the Miriam O'Callaghan show on TV about ten years ago. I was in *Mrs Brown's Boys* at the time and Miriam asked, 'Now, you're playing a gay man – how do you feel, as a gay man, playing that role?'

Ma will go mad now, I thought, because now all the neighbours will know, but I answered the question honestly. Afterwards, when I looked at my mobile phone, I saw that there were a load of missed calls from my mother. I thought, I can't be dealing with this now. We were going out for drinks with Miriam and the crew and, anyway, it wasn't a conversation I wanted to have on the phone. I'm taking her for lunch tomorrow, I decided. I'll talk to her then.

The next morning, at 8 a.m., I was still in bed when the phone rang.

'Howya, Ma.'

'We need to talk.'

'Well, I'm bringing you for lunch today, so can we not talk then?' I said, stalling for time.

'Perfect, what time will you be up at?'

'I'll collect you at one.'

'I'll be ready.'

Uh-oh, I thought, that's done it. I drove up to her house and, before she could open her mouth, I said, 'Now, off we go into town.'

But she stopped me. 'I saw you on television last night. All I want to say is that you spoke very well and you were the best on the whole show.'

That was the end of the one and only conversation we had about me being gay.

A few weeks after highlighting my hair, Justin decided that it was time for the perm. He turned up on my doorstep once more, with a plastic bag full of stolen products to do the job. 'First things first – let's get your hair washed,' he said, grabbing my arm and leading me into the bathroom. After giving my hair a good scrub – a bit too roughly, I thought – he hand-dried it with the bath towel that he'd hung over the radiator. 'Now, go and get your Ma's curlers while I mix up this perm solution,' he said.

My mother had recently bought a set of heated Carmen rollers, but I couldn't use them because I knew she'd need them. She put them in every night before bed and slept in them, so that she'd have that just-set look the following morning. Instead, I brought back the big bowl of well-used pink foam hair rollers that she didn't use any more, and asked if they'd do. 'Yeah, curlers are curlers,' he said confidently. 'Sit on the edge of the bath and I'll put them in. You'll be the image of the bopping elf by the time I'm finished with you.' (Marc Bolan was known as the 'bopping elf' because he was so short.)

When the curlers were in, he started to slosh the perm solution, which he'd made up earlier, on to each curl. 'Keep your eyes closed,' he ordered. 'You'll be blinded if any of this stuff gets into them.' When he had finished, he said, 'Now, leave that in as long as possible to make sure it sets.'

I looked at myself in the bathroom mirror and screeched, 'I look like Hilda Ogden!' Hilda was a character in *Coronation Street*, and she always wore curlers. 'How many minutes do I have to leave these in for?' I asked. Justin had gathered all his belongings into the plastic shopping bag and now, kissing me on both cheeks and giving me a hug, he said, 'You don't leave them in for minutes. Leave them in overnight. The longer you leave them in, the longer the perm lotion has time to work. Take them out before you go to school in the morning and wash your hair. You'll be the image of Bolan. See ya!'

'Are you sure this will work?' I shouted after him.

'I'm merely offering advice based on my expertise as a hair stylist,' he replied. BANG, the front door shut behind him.

'But you're not a stylist,' I said to the door. 'You're only a trainee stylist.'

When he left, I thought about how I was going to sleep with a head full of rollers. Would they all stay in if I tossed and turned in my sleep? The last thing I wanted was a combination of corkscrew curls and dead-straight hair. At bedtime, I decided to put on one of my mother's hairnets over the rollers to hold them in place. I was looking more like Hilda Ogden by the minute. Even today, over forty years later, I still squirm with embarrassment remembering this ridiculous caper. Eventually I drifted off to sleep, thinking about the new corkscrew curls I'd have in the morning.

Next morning, I woke to the sound of my mother calling me. 'Rory, get up, you'll be late for school.'

I'll get up in a minute, I said to myself. The next shout from my mother was louder: 'Rory, I've your breakfast on, get up now!'

The thing is, I'm not good first thing in the morning. I never have been. And the idea of another long day in school made me want to stay in bed even more.

'Rory, are you up yet?' my mother yelled. 'Don't have me come up there and drag you out of that bed.'

I leapt out of bed. The last thing I wanted was my mother seeing me wearing her old curlers and her hairnet. I had planned to wash my hair before I went downstairs, but my father was in the bathroom having a shower, and I knew that after that he'd need to shave. What was I to do? In a moment of insanity, I decided to get dressed, sneak out of the house, go to school with the rollers still in my hair and take them out and wash it there. And that's what I did. I put my duffel coat on, pulled the hood up and crossed St Benildus' fields to go to school. As soon as I got there, I rushed into the toilets, took off the hairnet and pulled all the rollers out. So far, so good. There was nobody else in the toilets.

I turned on the tap and stuck my head under it. Shit, only cold water. Well, what is it they say? 'No pain, no gain'? The water was freezing. I dried my hair off on the roller towel on the wall and turned to look in the mirror.

'Holy sweet Jesus,' I gasped. My hair, instead of having corkscrew curls like Marc Bolan's, looked like an aul wan's set. It was all piled up on top and it sort of hung with a tilt to the left. Just then, a couple of my friends, Seán Dawson and Johnny Byrne, came into the toilets. 'What the fuck?' Seán spluttered. 'What happened to your hair?' By now I was a gibbering wreck. Johnny ran out of the toilets, only to come back with a gang of other classmates. 'I told you!' he said excitedly. 'Look at the state of him!' I couldn't even run away, because I was wedged up against the wall furthest from the door, as more and more boys pushed their way in to see the freak show.

'What's going on here?' a voice boomed. It was Brother Brendan, the head brother. He'd heard the almighty commotion and had rushed upstairs to find out what was causing it. 'You, Cowan,' he blurted, looking at me in amazement. 'Take that wig off immediately.'

I thought I was going to pass out. 'It's not a wig,' I stammered. 'It's a bad hair day.'

Brother Brendan ordered me to go home and not to come back until my hair was presentable.

I ran home, hoping to find some coins so I could go into Justin's salon to get my hair disaster fixed. I'd forgotten it was my mother's day off. 'Jesus, Mary and Joseph,' she gasped when she saw me, 'What happened to you?'

I came clean. I told her everything, and when I got to the part about using her old curlers, she slapped the arm of the chair she was sitting on, 'Oh don't make me laugh,' she said, wiping tears from her eyes. 'Oh, I must go and ring Eileen.' Eileen had to be told all the stories about me. To my embarrassment, Ma was hysterical with laughter. 'No wonder you sneaked off without your breakfast this morning,' she said between bouts of laughter. 'Now, don't you move. We're going down to Herman's in Dundrum to get that mess sorted out.'

She was still giggling when she finished the phone call to my auntie. 'Right, let's go and get a proper hairdresser to sort out your mess. Oh, Rory,' she laughed, 'if you had a bald bit at the front, you'd look just like that fella Larry out of the Three Stooges. Now pull your hood up. I don't want the neighbours talking about us any more than they do already.'

We walked down the hill to Dundrum. My mother said we couldn't get the bus because she couldn't stop laughing and the conductor and the other passengers might think she'd lost her marbles.

If I thought my embarrassment at school was bad, it was in the ha'penny place compared to how I felt in Herman's, the hair salon in Dundrum shopping centre. First off, my mother told the receptionist what had happened and how my hair had got to be like this and then she asked if it could be fixed. The receptionist couldn't stop laughing either, nor could the stylist who was to try and fix my hair. All the other staff members just had to come over to where I was sitting, pretending they were looking for something, and they walked away laughing too. Even the juniors were hysterical. My discomfort and scarlet face only made them laugh more.

Eventually they all settled down. The stylist who was tasked with fixing my hair said, 'There's no way of reversing that. I'll have to cut it short. It'll still be curly, but at least you'll be able to blow dry it every day and straighten it out.' Just then, the T. Rex song 'Ride a White Swan' came on over the salon sound system and everyone in the place burst out laughing again. I just wanted the ground to open up and swallow me. 'Cut it all off,' I demanded angrily, interrupting their laughter. Oh, the shame.

My mother was delighted I was getting my hair cut short. She'd been on at me for a couple of years – 'Cut that hair; you look like Rapunzel' – and I'd always ignored her. Now here I was in a hair salon, demanding they cut my hair. I'd never live it down.

EIGHT

Never Give Up on a Good Thing

The summer after Hairgate, my mother had been over the moon at my Inter Cert results and the fact that I'd got an honour in maths. 'You'll get a wonderful job in the bank,' she'd said, waving a bunch of flowers she had cut from the back garden. 'A job for life, that is, and they give their staff a mortgage at cheaper rates than the ordinary Joe Soap.'

To my mother, a job in a bank was the holy grail. I think it was down to the fact that her family were so poor that she'd had to leave school after her primary education. Back in the 1940s, when Ma was at school, secondary-school education wasn't free and her mother, a widow, couldn't afford to send any of her children. They'd all gone out to work when they finished primary school at the age of twelve or thirteen. My mother always felt that the jobs that were open to her never reflected what she might have had if she had got her Leaving Cert, which is why she'd been furious to receive a letter from St Benildus asking me politely to leave.

As I've said, I wasn't a nasty boy, but I was bold and disruptive. I loved my friends in school, but I hated learning and I was always giving cheek, ever since I'd learned that it could get me laughs. I was forever being sent home for the day because I'd given cheek to the teacher, and Ma would be furious, ringing the school and demanding, 'What are you sending him home for?' I liked learning things, just not on the school's terms.

For example, I hated Peig Sayers, so I got hold of the English translation of her account of her life on the Blaskets and cobbled together something – an early Google Translate! When we studied Shakespeare's *Julius Caesar*, I got a double album of Laurence Olivier playing the role and he and the other actors brought it alive. One novel I loved in school was *Wuthering Heights*. I'm a visual learner and I could see the wild moors and Heathcliff and Cathy. I was also very good at maths and it suited me. Unlike other subjects, I'd work my way methodically through a problem, thinking that the solution would arrive if I took one step at a time. I look at my nephews' maths books nowadays and I can't understand a thing, but in the seventies I could follow it. Mind you, when my mother spotted that I was good at maths, I had to find a way to get out of it, which I'll get to.

The letter from the school had been sent that summer to the parents of four pupils, including me, saying that, as we had now done our Intermediate Certificate exam, it would be better if we got jobs, and the school was not holding places for us after the summer holidays. The head brother had not taken the decision lightly, it went on, but because we were so disruptive in school, he felt it would be better for us, and the school, if we didn't come back.

My mother went ballistic. 'You little swine,' she screamed, as she laid into me. 'Getting yourself expelled from school! I would have given anything for an education and here's you throwing one away!'

I tried to explain to her that nobody gets expelled from school like that. 'They have to actually do something that gets them expelled immediately,' I said, 'like fighting or cheating in an exam.' It seemed to me that Brother Brendan just wanted our parents to get us into line and behave ourselves.

For the rest of that evening, my mother stomped about the house, slamming doors and presses and finally, when there was nothing left to slam, she'd taken to her bed, declaring, 'You can think about what other school you want to go to, because you're not leaving at fifteen years of age.' She'd always take to her bed when she wanted to think things through. She'd think and rethink the problem until she had a solution.

'I'm writing to the Minister for Education,' she announced the next morning. 'I'll tell him that you're entitled to an education and that the school has no right to throw you out,' she said, wagging her finger at me. 'The cheek of that brother,' she'd added, putting her hands on her hips and cocking her head to one side. 'If he thinks he's getting away with denying you an education, he's got another think coming!'

Her blood was in danger of rising to boiling point again, but Da calmed her down. 'You don't want to write a letter to the minister when you're in a bad mood, Esther,' he said, patting her on the arm in an effort to pour oil on troubled waters. 'We'll compose the letter together and we'll do it with clear minds.' Ma would always listen to him, so he wrote the letter of complaint on my mother's behalf to the Minister for Education, enclosing the letter from the school. The parents of my three friends rang the school and made appointments to see Brother Brendan, and, as I suspected, he told them their sons could come back to school if they behaved. Upon getting promises from the parents that their children would stop being disruptive, it was agreed they could come back. I wished my mother had done the same, because a few days later, the shit hit the fan. Apparently, the Minister for Education wanted to know what the Head Brother was thinking by sending such a letter. He demanded that I be readmitted to school in the September and warned that there would be consequences if such a thing happened again.

Word spread like wildfire about the school being reported to the minister. The last thing any organisation wanted was to come to the attention of the authorities, because then they'd examine funding, staff levels, results, all of which would cause more trouble than it was worth. My mother couldn't care less about the fuss. 'He was asking for it,' she said, pursing her lips. 'He's quick enough to send us letters when he wants the parents to donate twenty-five pounds per house for new curtains because the school hasn't got funding from the state to buy them.'

I couldn't let her get away with that one. 'Ma', I said, smiling sweetly, 'you refused to pay the twenty-five pounds. You gave me a letter to bring in, saying why you were refusing to pay it.'

'You're quite right, I did,' she replied, through clenched teeth. 'Education is free now. There's no need for donations to the school. Now, what do you want for your dinner? I can do you a stew or I can do you a nice bit of pork steak with mashed potatoes and peas.'

The subject was closed.

When the Inter Cert results came out in September, it didn't bother her that I'd failed Irish but had done well in English, history and geography. Nor did it bother her that I'd barely passed French. 'You won't be working in France, so you won't need French,' she said. The only thing she was interested in was my maths results. 'If you're no good at maths, you can forget about getting a good job,' she'd say. Her idea of a 'good job', at a time when jobs were scarce, was one in a bank, the civil service or a government agency. 'You'll have a job for life, if you're lucky enough to get one in any of them. And you'd never have to worry about being made redundant, or having the company close down. It's the best job in the world,' she advised me, 'but you need a good maths result in your exams.'

I didn't agree. I was naturally good at maths and found the subject easy, but I'd no interest in it. I'd get a sinking feeling every time she told anyone that I was destined to work in a bank. I couldn't think of a job I'd hate more, but she would be as proud as a peacock at the idea of a son of hers working in the bank. 'Our side of the family had nothing. Your uncles worked in the fields and cutting down trees. Your uncle Tom was a milkman and your uncle Peter was a builder. They worked hard,' she said once to me, staring into the fire, the flames reflecting in her sad eyes, 'but they could have done so much more if they had been able to go to secondary school. And that's why I want you to have the best education you can get. I want you to have every opportunity that I didn't have.'

And this is where my father came in. He might not have said much – he tended to let my mother's storms blow out – but he had a good instinct for the kind of work that might suit me. So the summer after I'd done my Inter Cert, he got me a part-time job in the EMI record shop on O'Connell Street. He was the trade union official for the workers in EMI, then one of the big five music companies in the world, and that's how he was able to get me a job in one of their shops.

I was passionate about music, and I loved working in that shop. To think, I was being paid £21.50 per week to do something I would do for nothing at home ... play records.

After the summer, when I went back to school for my final year, I decided I wanted to work in something to do with music. Being able to earn a living from my passion was too good an opportunity to miss. But when I said as much to our career guidance teacher, he just laughed. 'You're wasting your time thinking about working in that industry. You should look at getting yourself an office job.'

An office job? I'd rather die. 'I'll think about it,' I said dismissively, realising that nobody but me knew what type of job I wanted – apart from my dad, that is. My mother, the career guidance teacher and the other adults urging me to get a job in the bank might have had my best interests at heart, but they weren't offering me advice on how to get work in the industry *I* wanted to work in.

I've always followed my own path, so, I decided that I was going to listen to nobody and to try and work it so that I could get a full-time job in the record shop and hopefully be promoted within the company. I spoke to the manager of the shop and he said there was a job waiting for me just as long as I got my Leaving Cert. So now I had a job organised. All I had to do was work it so that my mother wouldn't get her dream of seeing me in a job in the bank. I had to make certain that would never happen.

On the day of my Leaving Cert maths exam, I decided that drastic action was needed. I went in, took the paper, put my number on it, answered a number of questions wrong and a number of questions right. I wanted it to look like I'd tried but failed. It worked. When the results came out, I was delighted to see I'd got an F. There was no way I was capable of getting a job in a bank now.

My mother's reaction was predictable: 'You failed maths?' she shrieked, her voice going up a few notches. 'Mother of God, please tell me it's not true.'

It was true, though, and it was also true that in the summer of 1977 I got the job I wanted in EMI's record shop.

'I can't think of a job he'd be more suited to,' Ma's friend Mrs Wiley said when she heard the news. My mother didn't agree. But it *was* a job I was suited to and I was promoted a number of times over the next seven years, until I was sales and marketing manager for EMI Ireland. And even though I had a lovely company car, expenses, and flights all over the world, my mother would still ask, 'When are you going to settle down and get a proper job?'

I might have been a bit unfocused in school, but I was capable of hard work, I knew that. When I worked in the record shop, any time I wasn't serving customers, I'd clean and tidy and arrange the record displays so that they looked just right. I also discovered that I was great at selling stuff. I was only sixteen when I started, but I quickly developed an instinct for knowing if a customer was looking to buy something or just browsing. I would also cross-sell: if they'd ask for the new album by some punk band, I'd say, 'We have that, but have a listen to this too ...'

I also used to do things that nobody else did at the time, such as taking deposits for records. Many music lovers would come into the shop and say, 'I'd love that, but I'll have to wait until I get paid.'

'If you give me a deposit, I'll hold it for you,' I'd say. It might only be fifty pence, but an album was £3.50 at the time, which was a lot of money then. I had a little book with a list of names and the deposits paid and it worked like a dream. When the manager asked me what it was, I told him. He said, 'That's a great idea. If they don't take it, they don't get their deposit back.'

One day there were no customers, so I decided to do a little tidy, taking all the records down and giving them a good dust. I was just keeping busy. Little did I know that the managing director of EMI Ireland, Terry O'Rourke, happened to be passing, looked in the window and spotted me polishing the counter. I was completely unaware of this at the time, but later, I learned that he'd been really impressed. He'd thought, Now, that lad is showing a bit of gumption, so when someone left, apparently he said, 'Ask that young fellow if he'd be interested in a job in telephone sales; he showed initiative.' Telephone sales involved selling new releases and the back catalogue from EMI to record shops on the phone.

I got the sales job and a few months later, when a job became vacant up in the EMI warehouse in Glasnevin, I got a job as assistant to the stock controller; then, when the stock controller left, I was automatically given his job. Stock control then wasn't like stock control now, with computer programs and instant order fulfilment. In those days, it could take weeks for an order to come in, so keeping an eye on stock was more complicated. Thankfully, I found it very easy. If I were a stock controller for Weetabix or Barry's tea,

I wouldn't have had a clue, but I knew a lot about music. I was young, in my early twenties by this stage, and I knew what was selling – and it was a job I found interesting, so I was good at it. I've always felt that if you like your job, you'll do it well.

When I began at EMI, we were still using a system of waiting until somebody ordered something and then getting it in for them, but it could take four weeks for something to come from the warehouse in Hayes in Middlesex, or from Germany. The stock controller of Polygram in Ireland was in his sixties, and he wouldn't have a clue who the newer bands were, so he'd be less likely to fulfil demand. I remember in particular one stock control meeting in 1979, at which all the managers were present. Cliff Richard's song, 'We Don't Talk Any More' was number one in the charts – at a time when being number one would mean sales in the millions – and we didn't have any stock of it. The same happened with Pink Floyd's album *The Wall*. 'Get ten in,' my boss said, but I saw that we had 20,000 orders for it! I eventually persuaded them to order the 20,000 plus another 200 to be on the safe side and I can still remember them saying, 'I hope we sell those two hundred.'

When I became stock controller myself, I decided on a more aggressive sell-in. I had a formula: if reorders started coming in in the first week of a record's release, then we'd put in a big bulk order, because the stuff was selling, even if there was still a lot of stock out there in the shops. So, when the big reorders came a week later, I'd have stock there to meet the demand.

In my first year, 1980, John Lennon was killed and Beatles and Lennon records started going mental. We had to make sure that we had all the back catalogue in stock, because we knew the huge sales would only be in a short space of time. We were right. We sold everything in the two months after Lennon's death: after that, things just moved on, as is the way in the music industry. Then, I was young and interested in the music. I still am, but everything changes; I wouldn't be able to do it now – I wouldn't know the current stuff, even though I have boxes full of records. I love to go into Tower Records on Dawson Street with a big list. If you're really into music, it's like being Charlie in the chocolate factory!

Working for EMI also exposed me to classical music for the first time. Maureen Storey, the manager of the classical department of the music shop McCullough Piggott, was a great help. She was a tough cookie, but she knew her stuff. We'd always had trouble with keeping classical records in stock, so I took her out to lunch and asked her, 'What stuff in our catalogue should we always carry for you? Now, don't leave me with stuff,' I warned her. 'If I'm left with it, I'll never take your advice again.'

'Give me a week,' she said, and she took the EMI catalogue and highlighted everything that she thought worthwhile. 'Now, if you keep three or four of each of them, they'll always sell,' she told me. True to form, our share of the classical market went way up, because we never went out of stock of these titles.

At EMI, I felt I was the luckiest man in the world, doing a job I loved and regularly being promoted. At the time, artists' back catalogues were a big deal, and we were constantly selling out of bands like Smokey or Kenny Rogers, so to incentivise buyers, I used to go to the shops and say, 'If you buy ten, I'll give you an extra one free.' When I became sales and marketing manager, I was given carte blanche to sit down with the artists and their managers to discuss what we could do to promote them. If they were including Ireland in their tour, I'd assume that they wouldn't just fly in in the morning and fly out again that night; they'd arrive a few days before and relax, and while they were here they'd like to see their profile all over the place – in window displays and posters and whatever else I could do for them, such as ordering in plenty of merchandise. Quite often, artists' managers would take a walk around town and they liked to see their artist's picture everywhere.

Sometimes, I'd be creative and if the law got bent a little, I never minded. When Tina Turner came to Dublin I had a huge banner put up on a bridge in Drumcondra, on the way into the city from the airport: *Welcome to Dublin, Tina Turner*, in three-foot-high letters. The only thing was, our banner was obscuring the Guinness ad that was normally on the bridge, so they weren't a bit pleased – but we got a few hours out of it. Sometimes it went wrong, though. I can still remember getting into trouble for pasting a poster of Tina Turner onto the window of what I thought was a derelict building, but which was, in fact, the blacked-out window of an undertaker's in Phibsborough. You can imagine what they made of it, turning up to work the next morning to a huge poster of Tina, complete with leather jacket and cleavage. And I wasn't the only one who made mistakes with posters. A colleague of mine in Warner Brothers put a poster advertising Chris Rea's album *The Road to Hell* in the bus shelter right outside Glasnevin Cemetery.

But Kate Bush was my finest hour at EMI. Everyone of a certain age remembers Thom McGinty – The Diceman, as he was called – who would stand on Grafton Street doing mimes and performance art. He'd stand absolutely still or do a silly walk and his costumes were legendary. He was a Dublin institution and when he died in 1995, his coffin was carried down Grafton Street to a standing ovation.

Thom used to do advertising for local businesses – in fact, he got his nickname advertising a shop called The Diceman. At the time, Kate Bush was about to release a new LP (that's a long player, for you millennials). It was called *The Sensual World* and I wanted something really different to promote it. I approached Thom and asked him, 'Would you do something on Kate Bush for me?' I left the details to him, because I knew he'd do something memorable. The next day, I could hear her music blasting up Grafton Street – and there was Thom, done up like Pierrot the clown, with his hair straight down on one side of his head and stuck up on the other. He was pulling a child's toy trolley, with Kate Bush album covers arranged artistically on it, slowly walking up and down Grafton Street, songs from the LP filling the street. I'll never forget it.

I also got the pavement artists who worked on College Green and St Stephen's Green to draw the album cover for me and when I sent the marketing and sales report back to the UK, the word came back, 'Kate loves that!' I was chuffed, as you can imagine. At the time, loads of record shops just did window displays of album covers and posters and I thought, that's boring, let's try something different. The great band Talk Talk had an album called *The Colour of Spring* out at the time and I asked a talented window designer called Yvonne Farrell to do something unusual for me. She did – every branch of Golden Discs had tree branches and other spring-like decorations in their windows. And the album sold very well.

Ma was still doubtful about my choice of career. It was only in 1988, eleven years after I started working full time for EMI, that she admitted she thought I was doing well.

She was a huge Cliff Richard fan and in 1988, Cliff played his first concerts in Dublin since the late sixties. I took my mother to one of his shows, and as I had already arranged to take Cliff to dinner afterwards, I invited my mother to join us. She was ecstatic, and when we got to the Trocadero restaurant, we saw that Nana Mouskouri, the Greek singer, was there too. At the time, she was at the top of her game and had just performed that night. We asked her to join us and my mother was in her element. I put Cliff and Nana sitting beside each other and my mother sat opposite them. They talked about how they managed their diet on the road. Cliff said that he ate nothing before a show; Nana said she liked to eat a banana beforehand, to give her energy. My mother recommended a good fry-up to start the day and before I knew it, they were talking to each other about how they prepared food at home and what supplements they took, my mother chatting away like a contented budgie. She had the time of her life and she got photos taken with Cliff and Nana. We said our goodbyes to the two entertainers and as I was driving my mother home, she said, 'You're doing very well in that job. I'm glad you didn't go for a job in the bank.' And after that she apparently told anyone who asked, 'My son Rory has a great job in a record company and he's doing very well.'

Like every Irish mammy, mine wasn't thrilled when I moved out of home for the first time. Not that she even noticed for a while – I was two years out of the house before she realised that I'd left! My first place was a dingy, horrible bedsit on the third floor of some place in Rathmines, but I still used to go to Ma's for dinner every evening, with my dirty washing, like every young man at the time, and Ma was under the impression that I was still living at home because I'd appear every evening. She didn't have a clue that I was living elsewhere. Not a clue.

One argument we had at the time ended with her parting shot: 'When you're living under my roof ...'

'I'm not living under your roof,' I replied.

'What do you mean?'

'I live in Rathmines,' I explained.

She went mental, of course, to think that I was paying 'some guard, because it's them that own bedsits. You're paying a guard's mortgage.'

Trust Ma to have the last word!

When I was sales and marketing manager of EMI, I moved up in the world, and into a luxurious apartment, a massive place with two huge bedrooms, a big kitchen and bathroom and a balcony out the back, just over the bridge at Milltown – I couldn't afford it now! Myself and my old friend Annette Carroll (of Carroll's gift shops) rented it together. I moved in with Annette and my mother couldn't believe it.

'Come down and have a look,' I suggested to her one day. 'See where I'm living.' I wanted to show her that I was a success, in spite of failing maths in my Leaving Cert. But she wouldn't set foot in it, because I was 'living in sin with a girl'. Annette and I used to fall around the place laughing at Ma's misreading of the situation. Even when Annette got married, Ma would say, 'That could have been you.'

Even though she 'knew', in a manner of speaking, that I was gay, she still persisted in setting me up with girls. Every wedding in those days was torture because Ma would hunt down some poor girl to pair me up with. Annette and Colm's wedding stands out for me. I can still remember her saying, 'Rory Cowan, have I got a girl for you.'

All my friends cheered and laughed and broke into a chorus of 'Rory, Rory, Rory', and loud comments of, 'G'wan, you stallion ya' came from around the room. I gripped my champagne glass so tightly it nearly shattered and my face went deep scarlet. Not that my mother noticed – or she made a very good attempt at pretending she hadn't.

My mother barged across the room towards me, dragging some poor girl from the groom's side of the family. 'Rory, this is Niamh, and she's not married either. Niamh, this is my son Rory. Oh, there's Annette's mother. I must go and say hello.' And off she went, leaving Niamh blushing and looking as mortified as me.

This was far from an isolated incident. My mother had done something similar at every family member's or friend's wedding. On the way to every one of these weddings, she'd say, 'This year I hoped it would be you getting married to a nice girl.' Until I was twenty-one, there was no girl good enough for me in Esther's eyes, but her standards dropped with every year that passed after that! At Annette's wedding, I was now at the stage where a girl with a harelip, a gunner eye, a hunchback and a club foot would be suitable marriage material. Esther was prepared to look past outward appearances to see the beauty inside. If a girl was unmarried, it didn't matter why – she was still a potential daughter-in-law.

As it turned out, Niamh wasn't bad at all. She had a great personality and a wicked sense of humour and we bonded over our shared situation – her mother was also trying to fix her up with a man. In the beginning, her mother had wanted Niamh to marry a man who worked in a pensionable job, like a bank or the civil service, but her standards had dropped too: at this stage, it wouldn't have mattered if the potential husband was on the dole and had never worked a day in his life.

Niamh looked at me and said, 'I'm guessing you're gay, so nothing's going to happen with us, so why don't we just get the drinks in and have a laugh?' And that's exactly what we did.

Annette and Colm were made for each other and their wedding day was fabulous. Well, to everyone except my mother. She spent the whole day practically beating her breast because I was (a) not marrying Annette, and (b) not getting married to anybody. During the church service she kept nudging me in the ribs and whispering, loud enough for everyone to hear, 'That could have been you. If only you'd have made an honest woman of Annette. It serves you right, you can't expect to live with a girl without putting a ring on her finger. No decent girl is going to live with a man if he doesn't make his intentions known. You thought you could have your cake and eat it too. Well she found someone else, didn't she, and you've nobody to blame except yourself.'

I'd say Ma was the only person at that wedding who didn't know I was gay!

NINE

In My life

In the 1970s illegal drugs had taken over from polio and TB as parents' main cause of concern for their children's health. The last thing they wanted was for a child of theirs to be on drugs, including my mother, who put it to me in her usual inimitable way: 'You stay away from drugs,' she warned me. 'That's how Marilyn Monroe started and look how things turned out for her. Poor woman had everything and the tablets drove her to take her own life. And she was beautiful looking. So let her be a lesson to you.'

It's amazing how, in just a few short years, attitudes to taking pills had changed. Back in the sixties, there was a lot of ignorance about medicine and medication. Home cures were favoured. Nobody really knew about overdoses or taking tablets without a prescription. When I was a child, women used to swap tablets: 'These blue ones are great for taking the edge off,' one woman would say.

'Oh, give us a couple of those, will you?' the other would reply. 'The red ones I have are shite. They wear off too quickly.'

Valium, which was a new drug in those days, and antidepressants were handed out, or swapped between neighbours, almost like sweets. As long as the tablets kept what was then known as 'the nerves' at bay and took the edge off, that was all that mattered, and this was all thanks to … the medical card.

In the sixties, if you had a medical card, you became everyone's best friend. You could take your neighbour's symptoms to the doctor, present them as your own, and he'd give you a prescription, which you'd fill and hand over the medication to the neighbour who couldn't afford to go to the doctor, but who didn't qualify for the medical card. The same applied if you had a sick child and you couldn't afford to go to the doctor; a neighbour would oblige, taking his or her child to the doctor and describing 'their' symptoms. There must be thousands of people in Dublin with medical histories that aren't theirs! The neighbour would usually hand over the price of ten cigarettes to cover the cost of the person's trouble. Everybody was happy with the arrangement and nobody thought they were involved in anything dangerous. (Mind you, at that time it wasn't seen as wrong to rub gin or vodka over the gums of a teething baby to ease its pain!) Valium and antidepressants weren't seen as drugs: they were just a little help to get you through the day.

Around that time, there were a few people in the Dundrum area who had been convicted of being in possession of illegal drugs. Of course, the details of who they were and where they were from spread like wildfire. If anybody was convicted of any crime, it was reported in the newspaper, which might explain my mother's fear of my name ending up there.

There were hardly any drink-driving cases either, because garda checkpoints were few and far between. Back then it seemed that everybody drank and drove: 'I don't know how I managed to get home last night'; 'I looked out the window this morning to see the car parked sideways'; 'I had to drive with one eye closed to stop me seeing double' were common boasts. Nobody really understood the seriousness of drinking-driving.

One night in 1984, I was coming home from a popular nightclub in Dublin, the Pink Elephant, where I was a DJ. It was my side-hustle; because I was passionate about music, having the chance to play for an audience was fantastic. After a few pints while I was working, I'd settle down for a few more drinks after closing with the rest of the people working there.

On this particular occasion, I set out for home at about five o'clock in the morning. My car, an EMI company car, was outside the club. It never even dawned on me that I could lose my job if I lost my licence for drink-driving. There was a joke doing the rounds then, about a group of lads leaving a pub at closing time, and the punchline was: 'Let him drive, sure he's far too drunk to walk.' Well, that was me that night. Today, I wouldn't even think about driving if I'd had even one drink, but back then we didn't really know any better.

I put my case of records in the back seat of my car and got ready to drive home. 'The Pink' was in South Fredrick Street, and to head home I had to drive past Dáil Éireann in Kildare Street. There was always garda security there, twenty-four hours a day, every day. How I even thought it was a good idea to drive in the state I was in, and past the Dáil, I don't know.

I'd only turned the corner into Kildare Street when I saw a garda checkpoint about a hundred yards ahead. Because it was a one-way street, I couldn't turn the car around and go another way, and it didn't help that the tree I swerved to avoid was, in fact, the pine air freshener hanging from my rear-view mirror. The gardaí were not going to need a breathalyser to prove I was over the limit.

I was pulled into the side of the road by this huge copper. He looked like something that had been lured out of the Kerry mountains with a hunk of raw meat, as Brendan Behan might say. He indicated to me to lower my window.

'Have you been drinking?'

I thought it might be best to admit to a little drinking – in those days, you could legally drive after drinking two pints. 'I've had a couple,' I said squirming in the car seat.

'A couple?' he crowed, his voice rising with merriment. 'Well, if I was to breathalyse you, do you think you'd pass?' He was clearly delighted that I'd come along to give him something to do. I thought to myself that the only way I could pass a breathalyser test was if the Pink had been watering down their drinks.

'Look,' he said seriously, 'I know you're over the limit and you know it, too. Now there are people waiting for you at home. If you wrap this car around a lamppost and get killed, it's not going to make their lives better. The best thing you can do is to park your car over there and collect it tomorrow, when you've sobered up.'

Well, I couldn't believe what I was hearing. 'How am I supposed to get home?' I exclaimed like a fool, not seeing that I was being given a way out. 'This is a load of shite.'

'Listen, lad,' the garda said, completely unruffled by my outburst, 'I don't care how you get home. There are many options you can choose from, but driving this car isn't one of them. Now, leave the car there, like a good man, and go home.'

I was incandescent with rage, both with myself and with this poxy jobsworth of a garda who was making me walk the eight miles home. But I took it quite well, considering. I parked the car, got out and slammed the door. I opened the back door and took out my cases of records, and slammed that door shut too. Then I made a big deal of flinging my records into the boot and slamming that shut. Buttoning up my coat and flinging my unusually long gold-coloured scarf over my shoulder, I flounced off towards home. Looking back, I can see that the garda was very lenient with me. It wouldn't happen today.

When I told a couple of my friends the next day, they were outraged at the injustice of it. 'You should report him,' one of them said. 'If he didn't breathalyse you, he can't prove you were drunk, so you can claim he reefed you out of the car.' That idea was bounced about a bit between the three of us. We concluded that I would get compensation for police brutality and the garda who had brutalised me would lose his job. And for about five minutes we were delighted with the plan we concocted, but the reality was that I'd been driving while drunk.

After my little escapade, my and my friends' attitude changed. One of my best friends, Seán Dawson, is teetotal. So if we were at a house party, of which there were many, we'd ask Seán to drive home on his motorbike before we left. When he got home, he would ring us to advise us whether there was a checkpoint, and if there was, he'd tell us exactly where it was, so all the drivers who had drink taken would drive home by a different route. You can see why there were so few court cases relating to drink-driving.

Court cases relating to drugs were quite rare too. Mostly they were for possession of dope, with a standard fine of £5 if you were found guilty.

When the newspaper headlines in the mid-1980s screamed *Junkie George has eight weeks to live*, my mother's first reaction was, 'His poor mother.' Everybody, from children to teenagers to adults and the older generation, loved Boy George, the frontman of Culture Club. He had an amazing charisma and people really cared for him. I was a big fan too.

Of course, I laughed at my mother's comment, saying, 'It's him you should be sympathetic towards. He's the one with a serious drug problem.'

She wasn't amused. 'You're not on drugs, are you?'

'No, Ma, I'm not,' I said.

But I got what she meant about Boy George's mother. At the time, drugs were a new danger and all mothers were terrified their children would become drug addicts. My mother, and probably millions of others, empathised with Boy George's mam.

I was telling her the truth, kind of. I'd tried acid twice and hated it both times. The first time was in 1976. A group of us, myself and Justin included, had got some and we went into St Stephen's Green to take it. A few years earlier, it had been a treat to be taken to the very same park to feed the ducks, and now here I was, about to partake in the dreaded lysergic acid diethylamide – LSD.

The guy who'd scored the acid showed us his stash. It looked like little squares of blotting paper, but that's the way it works. Acid is a liquid and a drop is put on a bit of blotting paper. I thought this was a swindle. You couldn't even see the drug you were supposed to be taking. For a fiver, I was expecting more than a bit of blotter. But still,

Justin and I were inquisitive about the drug, so we handed over the money.

The lad dishing out the drug asked us to stick our tongues out and he put one piece of blotting paper on each of them. For about ten minutes, I thought we'd been conned. I didn't feel any different. When I'd tried hash, the effects were immediate. Two pulls off a joint and I'd be a slobbering wreck, sitting there trying to hold my head up to stop myself drooling all over my shirt. It's not a nice look. I wasn't mad about hash: while other people would get chilled and giggly, I would get totally stoned and my only contribution to a conversation would be to grunt.

Then something very strange happened. I noticed that one of the trees had a royal-blue leaf, and when I studied it, I saw the other leaves were changing, too, from green and shades of red and brown to the same royal blue. I could actually see these colours morphing in front of my eyes. This isn't bad at all, I thought, I could get to like this wonderful drug. Then someone said, 'Here, look! The drops of water are all different colours.' We were sitting at the duck pond in a quiet part of the park overlooked by the Shelbourne Hotel. We all rushed to the water's edge and did exactly what he was doing; scooping up water with our hands – right enough, as the water slipped through our fingers, the drops were made up of different psychedelic colours. God knows what we must have looked like to any passers-by, oohing and aahing while dipping our hands into the water and splashing it up into the air.

For a half an hour, this was great fun, but then I started to get bored. I took myself off, thinking that a walk would bring me back to normal. Not a chance! When you take acid, you can trip for up to eight hours. It doesn't stop. The feeling of normality might come back, but then the acid takes over again and you're back into the unknown. I was due home for my tea a few hours after I took the tab. I couldn't go home while I was tripping. I wasn't far enough out of it not to know that my mother would go apeshit if she saw I was on drugs. So I decided to walk around the city until the drug wore off.

After a while, I saw the most beautiful step I'd ever seen. I'll have a nice little sit-down on that gorgeous step, I thought. So I sat down and looked at the wall on the building opposite, up along the bricks to the roof and up again to the clouds. I studied the wall and clouds in detail. They kept morphing into different colours and shapes. I wanted this experience to stop. I tried to ask for help, but all the people around me looked like they were from Dickensian times, with barefoot children running around dressed in rags. Teenagers who would be at home in Fagin's gang were encouraging me to hang out with them. They all scattered when the police came along in their blue uniforms and tall hats. Women wearing bonnets, shawls and dresses down to their ankles were trying to sell flowers from big baskets. I knew this wasn't reality, but I can still visualise the whole scene. It was like something you would see in a film like *Oliver*, *Scrooge* or *My Fair Lady*. God, I just wanted that trip to be over. 'Lucy in the Sky With Diamonds' this was not. I was in the middle of a horrible experience that I couldn't get out of.

Maybe a nice little sleep on my beautiful step would help, I thought, and somehow I nodded off. When I came to, I saw that I was in a lane near the old Mercer's Hospital, behind St Stephen's Green. The smell of piss would have knocked a horse sideways at twenty paces and there was rubbish everywhere. It was an old cobbled lane with derelict buildings on either side of it. The step I had thought was the most beautiful step I'd ever seen was just a crumbling old piece of granite that had seen too many bad winters and had been neglected for years. When I stood up, a few pennies fell out of my lap. Passers-by must have thought I was homeless. I was mortified. Gathering myself up and dusting myself down, I headed home, swearing to myself that I'd never touch acid again.

My promise wasn't to last. The next trip I took was with friends at a gig in the Sportsman's Inn in Mount Merrion, when somebody offered us some acid. Well, it was night-time, so I could go home to bed when I got bored with it, I thought. I also didn't want to be left out and be considered an anti-drug prude. So we took a tab each. This experience was different. When we left the club it was dark, so I kept getting flashes of colours shooting past my eyes, but these splashes of colour were just flashes. I tried to catch them in my hands, but they were too quick for me. Needless to say, my mates, who were also tripping, thought this was hilarious. But I hated this trip more than the first one and from that day to this, I haven't taken LSD again. All it does is turn people who are on it into zombies. Also, if you're tripping on acid, everybody who sees you knows you are on something – there's nothing discreet about it. But it was the being out of control I hated.

Justin, on the other hand, who took his first trip with me in St Stephen's Green, was different. He thought acid was the best thing ever. I can still remember meeting him in town one evening after he finished work in the hairdresser's and we went to the Bailey in Duke Street for a drink. On the way, he told me how he couldn't wait to do acid again. Something walked over my grave and I shivered as I went up to the bar to get the drinks in. My gut told me that Justin was the last person in the world who should be taking drugs: he was already prone to mood swings, and I was afraid for him, but couldn't see what I could do to help him.

Justin turned eighteen in the summer of 1976 and took off to London, fulfilling his dream of seeing the bright lights of that city. I hoped things would work out for him over there, but to be honest, I was relieved that he was going. What had once been harmless pranks had started to take on a more sinister edge, and when he started to talk about breaking into houses and buying and selling acid and hash, I became wary. I was starting to avoid him and instead of seeing him every day, as I once had, we were now only meeting up maybe once a week. I was still only sixteen at this stage, and with my new job in the record shop and later in EMI, 'I can't, I'm working' became my excuse for not being able to meet up with him. I think we'd just grown apart, but I was the lucky one, I think now, that drugs had little appeal for me.

'Is there something wrong with Justin Rooney?' my mother asked me one day. 'He doesn't look like he's all there. Has he been taking drugs?'

'No, he hasn't,' I lied.

My mother was no fool. 'Then why do his eyes look funny, like he's up to no good?'

'He's not been well. I think he's on antibiotics,' I said, improvising, but Ma wasn't having any of it.

'Antibiotics, my backside. Rory, he doesn't look the full shilling and he's going around like a tramp. You be careful he doesn't lead you into real trouble.'

Justin had started to really get into drugs at this stage, and the people he hung out with were also taking drugs, people with whom he had absolutely nothing in common – except for taking drugs. Even worse, he started dressing like them. He'd once been a smart dresser, but now he wore tie-dye T-shirts day in, day out; old, faded bell-bottoms; and an Afghan coat that stank to high heaven when it rained. And it wasn't just his clothes: our heroes, Marc Bolan and Bowie, were 'boring' now. Instead, it was the Grateful Dead and Pink Floyd's *Dark Side of the Moon* that turned him on.

'Now, don't be disappointed when you get to London and you find out that Big Ben is a clock,' I laughed, when he announced he was leaving Dublin. He didn't find that funny. His sense of humour had been replaced by weariness. I can still remember his dad saying to him a number of years later, in 1984, 'Justin, why don't you get a job?'

'Because I'm tired, Dad. I've been tired since 1977.' I thought it was hilarious at the time, but looking back, it seems so sad, because he must have been in a very bad way. Justin's 'tiredness' was probably depression, but at that age, and at that time, nobody knew much about the illness.

We were having a farewell drink in the Sandyford house. Justin was getting the boat to Holyhead the next day. 'You could come over for a weekend, or a holiday?' he said hopefully.

'Maybe,' I replied non-committally, 'but if I'm going anywhere for a weekend break, or a holiday, I'd probably go to Spain. I like the idea of a place where nobody asks any questions if you go to bed in the middle of the afternoon.' I laughed, but he didn't seem to get it. He was gloomy and morose.

Things didn't work out for Justin over in London. Years later his mother told me that he couldn't hold down a job. 'His nerves were bad,' she said. I wasn't surprised to hear that he had mental health issues. Looking back, if he was suffering from some sort of depression, the acid and hash he was using wouldn't have helped. All I know is that he went from being a vibrant, entertaining, very funny teenager when I first met him, to a morose, humourless, low-spirited young man. And all in the space of two or three years.

Back then we didn't understand what depression was. A very good friend of mine is a sufferer and when I asked him to describe it, he said, 'If I had the choice between having AIDS or depression, I'd pick AIDS every time.' Now AIDS was a terrible disease, so to hear my friend speak in those terms stunned me, but it gave me an insight into just how bad genuine sufferers of depression feel.

Justin returned from England in 1984. He'd been taking drugs for a few years and while they didn't suit him, he kept taking them, until one night he took something and never came back to normal again. Whatever he took drove him over the edge. I later learned that he'd tried to take his own life in England and when he didn't succeed, he thought it was because the devil was keeping him alive. I went down to see him when he came home and was shocked. His eyes were sunken, with dark circles around them. He'd also lost a lot of weight and his skin seemed to be stretched tightly over his skull, making him look severely malnourished. He was very far from the Justin I'd known and loved and I felt sad at his deterioration. Without Justin, my teenage years wouldn't have been half as much fun and through him, I had learned that it was okay to be myself. I dread to think what my adolescence would have been like without him.

One Saturday night, on my way into town to meet my good friends Ken and Robert, I took a detour to Justin's house to see how he was getting on. His parents had gone away for the weekend and I'd promised them I'd keep an eye on him. The weather was fine, but cold, and the street and houses were in darkness. I stopped suddenly about three houses away from where he lived. I couldn't believe what I was seeing. Justin must have gone down to the church, or to a number of churches, and stolen all their candles, because his front garden was full of little white church candles, all lit and glowing in the night. When I got to the house, the front door was open and the sitting room was full of large altar candles. Dozens of them were lit around the room. The top of the piano was covered with masses of lit devotional candles in their little jars and there was Justin, dressed only in a towel, playing the piano and singing an old song, which must have been a favourite of his mother or grandmother.

It was a desperately sad and disturbing scene, but I tried to pretend there was nothing wrong. 'Howya, Justin,' I said cheerily, as I walked around the room, making sure there were no candles burning anywhere near flammable objects like curtains or books. I picked up a glass of water that was sitting on the top of the piano and drank it, wishing it was vodka. Justin picked up the empty glass I had left back on the piano. 'Holy God,' he said in a pious voice, looking up to heaven, 'did you drink my water?' I didn't know where to look. I was mortified for him and felt so sad that he'd ended up like this, but I also knew that this was something way beyond my ability to control. 'I'll leave you to get back to your singing,' I called over my shoulder and I hurried out the front door, feeling frightened and uneasy.

A few months later Justin tried to kill himself again. When I went to visit his mother and father at home, they were beside themselves with worry. 'What would make him do something like that?' his father wailed. 'Killing himself is not the answer. He could talk to me. If he's in trouble, I could help him.' Mrs Rooney just sat in her chair rocking backwards and forwards. Both of them looked like their world had fallen apart.

I knew that Justin wasn't out to his parents and I thought that maybe he might be finding being gay an issue. I explained to Mr Rooney that maybe Justin's problem was that he was gay and hiding the fact. Mr Rooney didn't say anything for a moment, his mouth open in shock. 'Well, surely something can be done about that?' he eventually said, staring at me with round eyes.

I gulped and said, 'No, there's no cure, Mr Rooney. That's the way he is.' It may seem surprising nowadays, but back then, people thought that being gay was an illness that could be cured.

Justin's father scratched his head. 'Why did he choose to be like that?' he asked.

I edged towards him. 'He didn't choose to be like that, Mr Rooney,' I continued uncertainly. 'It's how he is and it's perfectly normal.'

Justin's father stared at me in silence and then said softly, 'If that's the way he is, I'll try to understand. It won't be easy, mind, but I'll do my best.'

His wife stood up, smoothed down her frock and before her husband could change his mind, said, 'Right, let's go to the hospital. Rory, you'll come with us.' She said it in a way that implied I had no choice in the matter. It wasn't that I didn't want to see Justin, it was just that after that candle incident, I was afraid of what I might find.

The car journey was very quiet, with Mr and Mrs Rooney in the front and me alone in the back of the car. The silence was occasionally broken by Mr Rooney saying quietly, 'He's my son and I'll support him, no matter what he is.'

His wife patted his hand and I said in a cheery voice, 'That's the way, Mr Rooney, it'll do Justin the world of good knowing you love him and aren't going to disown him.'

We got to the hospital and when we walked up to the ward, Mr Rooney opened the door and stopped. Justin was sitting up in bed, propped up against two pillows, and sitting around his bed were a few very obvious queens. I knew them vaguely from the gay scene. One of them, with a fringe dyed the colour of Ribena and a T-shirt with a picture of Popeye's girlfriend Olive Oyl on it, looked at me and said, 'Hiya, girl, come and sit here on the edge of the bed.' I really wasn't impressed that he was referring to me as a female in front of Justin's parents. They were here to see their son, not get a lesson in gay-scene patter.

Mrs Rooney came into the room and took her scarf off. 'Ahem,' she said with a ladylike cough, 'which one of you *gentlemen* is going to offer me his seat?' She said 'gentlemen' in a tone that implied she was being ironic, but the lads did offer her a chair.

Mr Rooney's reaction was something else. He looked really fierce. 'Look at yous,' he said scornfully, 'you shower of nancy boys. What do you do all day?' It seemed that his earlier attempts at understanding had gone out of the window.

Mrs Rooney ran out of the room, sobbing and wringing her hands, without a backward glance. Well, I did my best,

I thought as I slunk out after her. The last thing I heard was Justin saying wearily, 'Oh, Daddy, can't you see I'm not well?' I didn't hear Mr Rooney's response.

Justin's mother was beside herself with worry. My mother knew some of the background because I had filled her in and when I mentioned that Mrs Rooney was very upset, my mother rang her and invited her up for tea and cake the next day. When she arrived at our house my mother gave her a hug, whereupon she burst into tears. My mother rocked the crying woman in her arms and, patting her on the shoulder, kept saying softly, 'There, there. Everything's going to be okay.'

While Mrs Rooney composed herself and my mother was waiting for the kettle to boil, she put the coffee table between the two armchairs and brought in a Victoria sponge. 'I hope you don't mind shop-bought,' she said, putting the cake in the middle of the coffee table, 'I just haven't had a chance to bake lately.'

Mrs Rooney just nodded and said, 'It's fine, Esther.'

My mother brought in the pot of tea and said, 'Will you pour, while I cut the cake?'

When they'd finished their tea and cake and had chatted about nothing in particular, my mother said, 'Tell me all about it.' She knew that what Mrs Rooney needed was for someone to listen. This wasn't going to be a back-and-forth conversation. Mrs Rooney was going to talk, my mother was going to listen and at the end she'd offer some comforting words.

Mrs Rooney gathered her thoughts and began. 'Justin was always a bit odd, but I closed my eyes to it.' And she was off. She gave my mother the full background, leading up to Justin ending up in hospital after trying to take his own life, adding that he was now in a secure unit.

My mother tut-tutted and nodded her head sympathetically at the right moments, and when Mrs Rooney had finished, she asked, 'Did they give you any information on when he'll be well enough to come home?'

Mrs Rooney sighed. 'We got a phone call last week from a Professor Lynch at the hospital. Very well spoken he was, as if to the manor born. "Modom," he said, "we've done all the tests we can think of on your son, Justin, and the results have come back. He's absolutely perfect. Whatever was wrong with him is gone now. He's perfectly healthy and his mind is as sharp as a tack. There's really no need for him to be here. He doesn't need to be here at all."'

My mother was astonished. 'Ah, that's great news. I'd say you were thrilled,' she said ecstatically.

'Oh, I was,' Mrs Rooney replied. 'The professor told me to come over and collect him immediately and bring him home.'

My mother looked slightly puzzled. 'So why is he still there?'

'Oh, we drove over,' said Mrs Rooney, in a tone that implied there was more to the story. 'And when we got there, we found out there was no Professor Lynch there. In fact, they'd never even heard of a Professor Lynch.'

It turned out that Justin had asked to make a phone call and then rang home. He'd put on a plummy accent and pretended he was a doctor. In spite of everything, the two women had a good laugh about this, and I couldn't help thinking that it was hilarious. There was Justin, locked in a secure unit in a home for the bewildered, probably on the best tranquillisers the then-Eastern Health Board had to offer, and he was still able to cause ructions.

In late 1986, Justin was found hanging from a tree in a wood near where we lived. He left no note. The last conversation I had with him had been difficult. He was home and I'd decided to call up to see him, but he had hardly recognised me and had decided to go for a walk in the middle of our conversation. I'm not sure if he knew who I was. I made my excuses and left. And that was the last time I saw Justin.

When I found out he had died, he was already buried. I'd been over in the UK on business and didn't get to hear about his death until I got home. The family wanted a no-fuss funeral, so there was no announcement in the newspapers, as there would usually be, and no mention of it in the daily Masses in the local church. As well as being heartbroken, the family were probably embarrassed that a loved one had taken his own life. So a quiet family-only funeral was what happened.

Back in the eighties, there was still a huge stigma around suicide. Many people considered it a selfish act to take your own life and leave your loved ones behind, with only questions to keep them awake at night and no answers to give them comfort or understanding. I wasn't surprised Justin had taken his own life, because he'd been so unwell, but I was surprised by the way he'd done it, which seemed so brutal. He had hung himself in a public place and his body was discovered by a person who was not a family member. God knows how many people saw the body between the time it was discovered and before the gardaí and ambulance arrived. Saying he died of natural causes was not an option for his family.

I remembered a time, soon after we first met, when we thought death was glamorous. We made jokes about suicide. Justin said once, 'I could go to the library and ask if they have a book on how to commit suicide. But the librarian would probably say, "Get lost, you won't bring it back."' Back then, we'd roared laughing. Now that he was dead, I just chuckled sadly to myself at the memory.

Initially, I thought that his life must have been miserable. Imagine believing you were possessed by the spirit of a dead person and that the devil was trying to keep you alive. His world must have been a horrible place to live in. Maybe you're better off out of it, Justin, I thought. But then I reasoned, no, you might have got better. To me, suicide is not the answer. If someone is released from suffering from a terminal illness, where there's no hope, it doesn't have to be tragic. Friends and family wouldn't want their loved ones suffering, I get that. But in the case of Justin and his psychological suffering, with the right help and medication and time, I think things might have got better for him.

I wish I could say that Justin's was the only suicide among my circle of friends, but it wasn't. Two brothers of a friend of mine killed themselves too, one a year or two after Justin and the other about ten years later. Two families each losing sons to suicide. How the parents must have felt doesn't bear thinking about.

Then, of course, there were my friends Joe and Derek, a couple I'd met on the gay scene. Joe took an accidental overdose and, a year later, Derek, unable to live without Joe, swallowed a couple of packets of paracetamol and died too. A school friend of mine threw himself into the Irish Sea off Dun Laoghaire pier soon after we did our Leaving Cert.

Eight people I knew took their own lives. The sad thing is that nobody's lives were better because those people weren't in them any more. And as for suicide being a 'selfish' act, I now understand that not one of those suicides was an act of selfishness. All eight took their own lives because of despair or sorrow. Their deaths were all totally unnecessary, though. With time and with help, I think the lives of those eight people could have got better.

My mother found Justin's death very upsetting. For a while afterwards, if I came home late, she'd be waiting up for me. She'd be sitting in her armchair with only the light from a lamp to keep her company.

The first time this happened, I was more than surprised to see her up at two o'clock in the morning. 'Why are you still up? Is there something wrong?' I asked urgently.

'I was just thinking about poor Mr and Mrs Rooney,' she said sadly. 'They're very respectable people and always led busy lives. They must be out of their minds, God love them.'

I nodded in agreement, wondering how they would ever get over their tragedy. 'You'd better never think of doing anything like that,' she warned. 'You were his friend. Do you know why he did it?'

'Ma, if I knew what drove him to it, I might have been able to stop it. Nobody knew what made him do it. Now would you like a cup of tea before we go to bed?' I was desperate to change the subject – it was too upsetting. She nodded that she would and I went out to the kitchen to boil the kettle and get the cups and milk out of the press and fridge. I didn't bother putting the light on in the kitchen because I knew my way around in the dark.

What was that? I knew I heard something behind me. It's not my imagination, I thought. I can definitely hear something that sounds like shuffling. Justin Rooney, if you've come back to haunt me, you can take a hike now. Don't be silly, I said to myself then, there's no such thing as ghosts. I couldn't turn around because I was rooted to the spot with fear. My heart was thumping and I could hear my blood pumping in my ears. A voice suddenly came out of the darkness. I screamed and turned around, gasping for breath with one hand over my heart and the other over my mouth.

'Switch on the light, for God's sake,' my mother said, yawning. 'There's a nice bit of chicken in the fridge if you want to make a sandwich.'

Trust Ma to break the atmosphere!

Looking back, this period of my life was tinged with sadness. I was forging a life for myself in EMI and as a gay man, but old friends like Justin would never live to forge their own lives. I learned a lot from my friendship with Justin: we may not have been close in many ways, but he was a rule-breaker, a man who was determined to do things his own way, just like me. He'd look at the rules and say, 'Forget that.' For Justin, the rules were there to be broken, just as they'd been when we'd spotted that wheelchair on the footpath on Dundrum hill. That was Justin all over: he was like a firework, burning bright, then fading away.

TEN

Make Your Own Kind of Music

At Christmas 2017, many years after Justin's death, I played a dame in the panto *Polly and the Beanstalk* at the Olympia Theatre. I loved the big hair and the outrageous make-up that I had to use to exaggerate my facial features. It took a while to get all the make-up on, but luckily I didn't have to do it myself; the production company provided a make-up artist. However, make-up was like a conveyor belt and you daren't miss your slot.

One afternoon, while I was in the chair in the make-up room, getting my slap on for the first performance of the day, one of the young dancers was waiting for his turn to get powdered up. He was talking to one of the other dancers and I overheard him mentioning that he had been out with his boyfriend the night before.

'Are you queer?' I asked incredulously. For once, my radar had malfunctioned, but I was going to have a bit of fun teasing this out-and-proud young lad.

He looked at me in shock, then he said proudly, 'I'm *gay*, not queer.'

'Well, back when I was your age, gay people were called queers,' I told him. 'More seriously, does your mother know about your condition?'

'I told my mother I was gay when I was fifteen,' he said defiantly, 'and it's not a condition. It's normal.'

'And how did you feel when she threw you out of the house for being queer?' I asked him. 'Back in the seventies and eighties, it was fairly common for gay people to be thrown out of the family home if it was discovered they were gay.'

He started to show interest. 'Why?' he said, sitting down in the chair next to me.

'For bringing shame on the family. That was actually a very common occurrence.'

Just then, the make-up woman asked me to lie back in the chair and close my eyes while she made them up. The dancer went and made himself a cup of tea. And while he was pouring the boiling water on to the teabag, he asked if I'd tell him about the old days. My eyes shot open. This kid must see me as an ageing old ham, a modern-day Methuselah, I thought, but I bit my tongue and remembered what the purpose of the exercise was: to explain to a young gay person what things were like for gay people in the past – what battles were fought so that people like him could be equal citizens today.

'Where do you want me to start?' I asked him. I explained that Ireland had gone through a massive transformation regarding gay rights. 'Before 1993, gay sex was illegal and you could face up to two years in prison. And if you were outed, you could lose your job, especially if you were a teacher, or if you worked in a hospital run by the religious orders,' I said.

'No way!' the dancer cried out in surprise, pausing for a moment to blow on his hot tea. 'You can't get sacked for being gay,' he said, looking at me suspiciously, as if I might be lying.

'Not today,' I replied, 'but not so long ago you could be.'

The dancer wrinkled up his nose in disgust and said, 'That's not right! That shouldn't have been allowed.'

'It's true,' I said. 'Some parents would be ashamed to have a gay son or daughter, so they'd throw them out of their home. And you could be beaten up and you could do absolutely nothing about it. You couldn't even go to the guards, because they would ignore the fact that you were assaulted and instead they'd concentrate on how you were breaking the law. Being gay was a good enough reason to evict you if you were renting a flat. Oh, a lot of gay people had to keep things very quiet for fear of what might happen if it was known they were gay.' I told them all this slowly

and quietly to let the facts sink in. Other members of the cast and dance troupe had come in by then, and they were all listening intently too.

'That's shocking,' said the dance captain, shaking her head in disbelief.

'Right,' I said, 'let's get this show on the road. When the matinée is finished, I'll tell you all how Brendan O'Carroll employed me *because* I'm gay.' (I'll tell you later too!)

It's true: that's precisely why Brendan hired me, and he was way ahead of the game, both in that respect and in the characters he created in *Mrs Brown*, who made being gay perfectly normal – even mainstream. But back in the seventies and eighties, being gay was far from that, and even though I credit the gay scene with some of the happiest memories of my life, hiding who you were from your family and society was incredibly hard. So many friends of mine didn't survive, and those who did have the battle scars to prove it.

While we might not be accepted by society at large, everyone was accepted on Dublin's gay scene: transvestites – or 'dockers in frocks' as we used to call them – would come in a bus to a gay bar and park outside; punks, goths, skinheads, all the minority groups would come to the gay bars, like the Viking and Bartley Dunne's, and be let in and accepted. One famous Dublin gangster used to sit in a corner in the Viking because he knew the guards or other criminals would never think to look for him there!

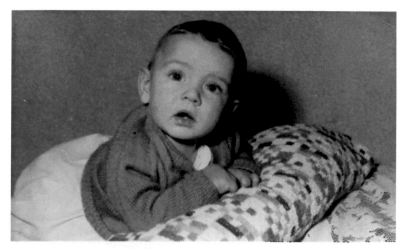

The moment you realise what you thought was a fart, wasn't. I was a gorgeous baby.

Three little ducks sitting in a row. Myself, Gerard and Maeve on a holiday in a caravan in Rush, County Dublin, in the mid-60s. This picture must have been taken early in the morning because we were spotlessly clean.

On the beach in Rush in the late 60s. L–R: My cousin Mary Doyle, me, my dad, Maeve and Gerard. Da was only in his 30s but at the time I thought he was ancient.

Ballybunion, County Kerry, 1970. Myself and Gerard posing on the beach. What am I like? Not a bit camp!

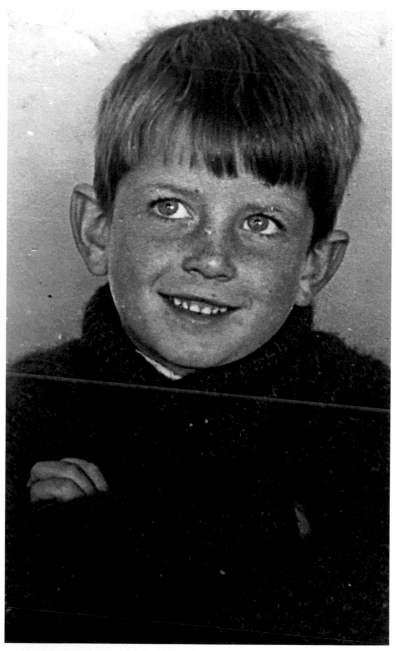

My school photo. I was about five or six. Cardigan knitted by Esther.
Probably the last time I looked angelic.

Athlone, 1970. The cast of the first school play I was in. Brother Anthony was the teacher and the show's director. I'm in the middle of the back row wearing a trilby hat.

Athlone, 1970. On the class football team. As you can see, I wasn't really into football, because I'm wearing my shirt under my football jersey.

It's almost fifty years since these photos were taken in the Marist Brothers school in Athlone, yet I remember when these weren't old memories. Immediately after these pictures were taken we got changed and went home for lunch.

Esther showing a bit of leg in Tel Aviv in the early 80s. Growing old is compulsory. Growing up is optional.

At my twenty-first birthday party. I had hair then. What I like about these photos is that they're proof that once, if only for an instant, everything was perfect.

My Da and his mother on O'Connell Bridge in the early 50s. He was only
about twenty years old then. Back then, children dressed like their own
dads when they left school.

At a party in the apartment I shared with Annette. There were always parties there. On the left is my old pal Ken Hutton wearing a sweatshirt I'd given him, advertising a Queen single. I'm beside him. I haven't a clue who the other three are. But that was parties back then. You never knew who was going to turn up.

The night I won the Miss Greenfields contest in the Canaries in 1993. The next night I came second in the Mr Macho competition.

Esther and her old friend Lily. Lily always hoped they'd find a cure for my condition. She didn't get the gay thing, bless her.

Ma and Cliff Richard, 1988. It was that night she eventually accepted I had a good job in EMI Records.

Me with the Pet Shop Boys.

Me with Paul and Linda McCartney.

Me with Tina Turner.

Me with Cliff Richard.

Me with Kate Bush.

I never thought I was good-looking, but when I look at these old photos I realise I was! They are over thirty years old and looking at them makes me realise how quickly time has passed.

With my Ma, a few weeks after I had my brain tumour removed.

At Annette Wall's wedding to Colm Carroll. L–R: James Bailie, Noel Palmer, Stephen Smith, Annette, Gary Kavanagh and me. Didn't we look smart. Annette, who my mother thought I should have married, looks gorgeous and happy.

The *Mrs Brown's Boys* gang heading to the BAFTAs. (© *Steve Vas/ Featureflash/Shutterstock*)

Mrs Brown's Boys only went and won a BAFTA.

Mrs Brown's Boys won so many comedy awards. Here's me with one of the National Television Awards the show won. What way was I smiling? It looks like my upper set of teeth are dentures and false gums.

As an ugly sister in *Cinderella* at the Tivoli Theatre, Dublin, 2014. I love doing panto. (© *Collins Photo Agency*)

With Esther. Dementia had taken its toll on her at this stage. But this was a very happy day. I'm looking at this photo and wishing I could go back to that day. She was so happy and content. (*Cathal Burke/VIPIRELAND. COM*)

A night at the theatre with Esther. People used to say I was exactly like her. Esther called it karma for something bad she must have done to end up with a bold son like me. (*VIPIRELAND.COM*)

The last time my mother came to see me perform on stage, SSE Arena, Belfast, 2013. I love this photograph. It was taken by Paddy Houlihan who plays Dermot Brown in *Mrs Brown's Boys*. We're all stories in the end.

Another customer was George, a shoplifter from Ballybough. He could steal anything, fur coats, suits, you name it. My friend Tom Kennedy from Alias Tom bought George a bottle of champagne to persuade him to stay out of his shop. George still walked out with a suit. His most famous haul was a wedding dress from Switzer's. It took him four days to get it off the mannequin and out of the shop window! George was also a great man for the malapropisms. He thought that 'Willie Mandela' was doing a great job in South Africa!

My favourite George story, though, was when he went to America, on the run from the guards. He'd driven to Cork and he'd then he'd driven back, stopping off in every shopping centre on the way back and stealing whatever he could get his hands on. He got as far as Portlaoise and was caught. They were only going to charge him with stealing a shirt, but then they saw his haul of stolen goods in the car. That was that! However, before his case came up for trial, George skipped off to the States, where he worked as a security guard in a big store in Chicago – oh, the irony! Now, this was around the time that the film *The Commitments* came out, based on Roddy Doyle's novel about a band trying to make the big time. Poor George went to see it and started crying. I want to go home, back to my granny's, he said to himself.

One day he was at work, and this wealthy woman had been on a major spending spree, her arms full of bags from the expensive store. George was told to bring it all to her car. He saw his chance. He got in and drove straight to the airport, got out of the car, taking all the expensive clothes and jewellery with him, and got on a plane, abandoning the car in the airport car park. His granny's in Ballybough must have looked like Aladdin's cave!

Another popular spot on the gay scene was Flickers, a gay disco in a building owned by members of the gay community in the Hirschfield Centre on Fownes Street. There was no drinks licence, so we'd smuggle in naggins of vodka in our cowboy boots. It was fantastic and I made some of my best friends there. Mind you, Gay Pride in those days was just a few people with whistles! They'd march on the streets and people would look on and the odd one would give you abuse, but most people supported it.

After a few years the scene gradually started to get bigger: Noel Palmer closed the Viking and opened The Parliament in what is now The Turk's Head pub, and he would host 'gaylies' in the top-floor function room. You might meet anyone there: politicians, doctors, lawyers and rent boys – in fact, the rent boys spent the most on drink. There was one guy, from Sean McDermott Street, who we used to call Hira, because he'd always ask the barman to raise the volume on the jukebox: 'Hira!' he'd say. On one occasion he bought a huge round of drinks – there must have been forty quid's worth on the tray – and tripped and fell with a clatter, glass and booze flying everywhere. 'Noel, same again please!' he yelled.

Of course, any gay man worth his salt has a fag hag, and I was no exception. A fag hag is a woman whose best friends are gay men, but who is not gay herself. They like gay bars and clubs because they can dance and have a few drinks without being hit on by straight men. Justin and I had a fag hag. Her name was Yvonne and she was outgoing and fabulous company. She was what was known as kooky: she made her own clothes and her red curly hair was so long it lent itself to being straightened or tied or brushed into the most fabulous eighties hairstyles.

There was never a dull moment with Yvonne. Whenever you met her she was always in the middle of some drama or crisis. She was the kind of girl who, if you bumped into her on the street and said, 'How are you?' she'd tell you, and you'd come away from the conversation delighted that you'd met her. Drama just seemed to follow her.

On one occasion, she invited me to a charity auction for a group called Friends for Friends, the first AIDS charity organisation in Ireland. At the time, AIDS was a new and deadly virus and if you contracted it, you died. Friends for Friends helped people with AIDS and their families with things like accommodation, doctors' bills, funeral expenses, basically whatever they needed to make their loved one's final days or months more comfortable. It was set up by a good friend of mine, James Bailie, and I supported it from day one. In my opinion, it was a fabulous charity and a really worthy cause.

James was from Northern Ireland and he was a Protestant. He was also one of the loveliest guys I've ever met. When I met him first, he had a flower shop in Duke Lane, just off Grafton Street. I commissioned him to make flower arrangements for any of the EMI acts who were coming to Dublin for concerts or to do promotion. The arrangements he made up were more like creations. I have never seen anyone who could work with flowers like he did. All the EMI acts commented on how lovely the flowers in their hotel rooms were.

In 1986 Queen were due to play at Slane Castle and had sold 80,000 tickets. They were supposed to be staying in the Westbury Hotel and got James to make up four flower arrangements and I bought four bottles of Cristal champagne to be sent to their rooms. It was all on my EMI expense account – I wasn't paying for all this out of my own pocket! In the end, only Brian May arrived. He was married to an Irishwoman at the time and they had come a few days early so that they could visit his wife's extended family. The other three members of the group were going to fly in on the morning of the concert, get helicopters from the airport to Slane and then back to Dublin after the show, before flying back home to London. I sent the flowers and champagne to Brian May's suite in the Westbury, but what to do with the other three flower arrangements and bottles of champers? The flowers I brought up to the children's hospital in Crumlin, saying they were courtesy of Queen. The three bottles of Cristal I kept for myself and brought them home to the apartment I shared with Annette. We drank all three in a gluttonous session around the table. So, thank you, Queen, for those three bottles of Cristal!

James was affectionately known as Orange Lil and I only found out he was a Protestant and a Loyalist when we were invited to the house he shared with his partner, Sean O'Leary, on St Patrick's Day for brunch. As I stood in the front garden, another friend hung a large tricolour from one of the bedrooms. I didn't think anything of it. It was St Patrick's Day, after all, and the city would be full of tricolours, but then James came out with a drink in his hand and asked what was up. My friend just pointed up at the bedroom window. 'Which one of you Fenian bastards hung that flag out of my window?' he yelled. He was joking, really. He wasn't a stereotypical Northern loyalist: we slagged each other off and took the piss out of each other's religions. No offence was meant and none was taken. James was fabulous, a lovely guy and without him, so many gay men wouldn't have received a decent burial at home in Ireland.

A couple of years ago, Sean O'Leary died of cancer. James was heartbroken. On the first anniversary of Sean's death, James had a gathering in their house to celebrate his husband's life. The house, which was very big, was packed. It showed the high regard in which so many people held James and Sean. James gave a speech in which he said that even though a year had passed, he was still broken. That was the word he used – 'broken'. There wasn't a dry eye in the house. After most of the people had left, I spent some time with James, talking about old times. I left in the early hours of the morning, promising we'd meet up when he came back from a much-needed holiday. James died in his sleep in Spain. He was only sixty-two.

In the early eighties, many Irish gay men who contracted HIV went to the UK when they developed AIDS. They'd send word home that they had cancer. Many Irish families never knew that their loved ones were suffering from AIDS. It was a hard and sad time.

The auction that I attended with Yvonne came about because funds were needed after the funeral of a young man from inner-city Dublin who had died of AIDS. He was one of eight children and his family were working-class people who didn't have much money. Friends for Friends stepped in and told his parents that they would cover the funeral expenses. The only problem was that they didn't specify a budget, and because the dead lad's family was such a big one, and he had lots of good neighbours, the family assumed the cost of everything relating to the funeral was to be covered. They booked eight black cars and a beautiful oak coffin. They booked a choir to sing in the church and they had an open bar and carvery in the local pub for the afters. In the heel of the hunt, the cost of that particular funeral left the charity with next to nothing in its coffers. So James decided to hold another auction to try and get some money in. There were a couple of people who had died in England and their bodies needed to be brought home, so funds were needed by the charity to do this.

This auction was held in a church hall in Terenure. I was late getting there, but Yvonne had told me earlier that she would hold a seat up the front for me. When I got there, the auction was in full swing and, noticing me coming in the main door, Yvonne waved at me to let me know where she was sitting. The auctioneer thought she was bidding on a lot. 'Sold. One hundred pounds to the lady at the front,' he said, banging his gavel.

Yvonne let out a scream. 'Hold on, I wasn't bidding! I was waving to my friend. Tell them, Rory!' Everyone at the auction knew her and took the piss out of her, and being the great sport she was, she took it all in good spirits. 'All right, what did I buy?' she went on. 'I hope it's something I need.' You'd want to have seen her face when she found out she'd bought the use of a mini cement mixer for a week.

Yvonne worked as a window-display artist in Switzer's department store, which is now Brown Thomas. She was fantastic at her job. Her window displays were really eye-catching and she was famous for using natural, found materials, like branches, flowers and unusual fabrics. Her window displays were definitely original, but probably ahead of their time. Her boss, in particular, thought she was away with the fairies and didn't appreciate the artistic talent she brought to the window displays. He was always trying to get rid of her, but the other managers in the store liked her and liked her displays, so he couldn't get her out. Though it wasn't for want of trying. Later, I used her for my Kate Bush campaign, which was a great success.

We used to meet up a few times during the week for a drink at lunchtime. And one Saturday afternoon we arranged to meet in the Bailey pub on Duke Street, just around the corner from Switzer's, for a sandwich. The place was packed and, after lunch, Yvonne had to go back to work. I stayed on and joined a few other people I knew at the bar. A couple of minutes later, Yvonne came rushing back in. 'There's a bomb scare in Grafton Street,' she said excitedly. 'In Switzer's. The army are there now. All of Grafton Street is closed off and the store has been evacuated.' She was delighted she didn't have to go back to work. 'I hope they don't open the street until six o clock,' she chirped. 'Get me a glass of wine, will you? I need a drink for the shock. Look – my hands are shaking. I could have been in that shop not knowing there was a bomb.'

The all-clear was given about two hours later and Grafton Street was reopened to the public, but the closure had come at a cost of many thousands of pounds in lost revenue to the shops and bars on the street.

Yvonne had to go back to work. 'If they ask why I'm pissed,' she said, 'I'll tell them it was the shock of it all. I needed to steady my nerves.' And with that, she was off.

Half an hour later, she was back. 'I've been sacked,' she said.

'You weren't caught nicking stuff from the shop, were you?' I asked.

'Don't be smart. I was told I was lucky I wasn't being arrested and charged.'

'Charged with what?'

'Planting a bomb! Before lunch, I was working on a display in the main window. When I left to come and meet you, I forgot my handbag. I left it sitting at the edge of the half-finished window display.' Yvonne's handbag was a square metal camera holder. I started to laugh and she slapped me on the arm to shut me up. 'Someone reported it as being a suspicious object and the army bomb-disposal unit was called. They closed off the street and did a controlled explosion on my bag.' She was chuckling to herself at the absurdity of it all.

'Did they give you a reference?' I asked, roaring laughing.

Another friend of mine at the time was Frank McCann, bar manager of the Viking. Frank was from Cavan and had moved to Dublin when he left school. He was gay, but he wasn't out to his family. On one occasion, Frank's mother was coming to Dublin and as she was planning to drop into his workplace to meet all his friends, Frank panicked. 'You're all going to have to butch up,' he warned us. 'And you dykes are doing to have to look like women, not car mechanics and truckers. You leather queens, standing along the wall, looking bored, there'll be no leather on display on Friday when my mother is here,' he said, whisking the bar-food crumbs off the counter as if he was going to war against them. 'It's like a tannery in here sometimes,' he continued. 'At the weekends, there's enough leather and chains in here to clothe the Hells Angels and not one of you owns a motorbike. Well, not this Friday, okay?'

One of the customers interjected. 'Rosie,' he said tartly, using Frank's other name, 'We're not bringing leprosy to the bar. We're hardly going to infect your ma by wearing a bit of leather.'

'No leather on Friday,' Frank repeated, 'and if anyone calls me Rosie when my mother is here, you'll be barred for life.'

The name Rosie had been bestowed on Frank a few years previously, when he first arrived on the scene. It came from a line in an old Irish song, 'Star of the County Down', which went: 'Rosie McCann, from the banks of the Bann/ She's the star of the County Down!' The name stuck, so much so that many people on the scene only knew him as Rosie.

When Frank hit the gay scene in Dublin, he hit it running. He worked in it, socialised in it, and most of his Dublin friends were gay. He kept all this a secret from his family and friends back in Cavan. Once, during a bus strike, he wanted to go back home to Bailieborough for a few days and I offered to drive him there. It was only about sixty miles away and we were having lunch in the town before I drove him the couple of miles further to his family home. 'I won't bring you into the house, if you don't mind,' Frank said, blowing on a forkful of shepherd's pie and pointing at the bright yellow soft silk shirt I was wearing, which looked more like a blouse. 'They might ask too many questions.' He gave me a half-smile to show me he didn't mean to be unkind. 'This is Bailieborough and they don't have gay people here,' he explained.

They must equate it with good food, because they don't seem to have any of that either, I thought, as I pushed a bland piece of fish around the plate. What Frank had said didn't bother me, though. Back in the mid-eighties, very few people on the gay scene were out to their families, including me.

So Mrs McCann was coming to Dublin to visit the son she didn't know was gay in the gay bar he worked in, and we were all under orders to 'act normal'.

I tried to calm Frank down. 'Don't upset yourself, Rosie,' I said airily. 'Nothing will go wrong. Who else is working with you that night?'

Frank was as close to a gibbering wreck as I'd ever seen him. 'Lily Cleary,' he said, looking at me in dismay. I blanched at the very idea. Lily was from Limerick and I never knew what his real name was. He was Lily to everyone and he was outrageously camp. Lily's natural way of standing was with his knees slightly bent to the side, one hand on his hip and the other bent at the elbow with the palm turned upwards. If you've ever seen the film *La Cage aux Folles*, Lily would put you in mind of Jacob, the gay butler who went barefoot because he couldn't walk naturally wearing shoes. Well, Lily was like that. If he stood up straight with his arms by his sides, he'd probably fall over.

Frank and I had been to see *La Cage aux Folles* in the Film Centre on Burgh Quay a few weeks earlier and the plot of that movie was sailing a bit close to Frank's predicament now. In the movie the two gay characters try to pretend they are straight when they meet their son's prospective in-laws, who are very conservative. Frank was going one further – trying to pretend that a whole pub full of gay people were straight.

This reminds me – we were sitting in the cinema waiting for the film to start when in walked four young non-gay couples. By their conversation, we realised they hadn't a clue what type of film they were coming to see. The lads obviously thought that as this was a French film, with subtitles, it was going to be all sex and it might get the girls in the mood. About five minutes into the film, the lads were mortified and their embarrassment got worse when one of the girls said, at the top of her voice, 'Here, are you trying to tell us something?'

But back to Frank's dilemma: what to do about Lily Cleary? There was no way you could butch him up. Now Lily was lovely, a really nice, sweet guy, but he tended to drink too much, get even camper and loud in drink and he once told me he hadn't spoken to a straight person in two years. When I thought about it, I realised it could be true. Lily worked on the gay scene, lived in one of the flats over the pub that were all occupied by gay people, and he socialised on the gay scene. And as straight people didn't go to gay bars back in the late seventies, it was quite plausible that he could have gone two years, or more, without ever meeting a straight person.

'What are you going to do, Rosie?' I asked, trying not to laugh.

'Oh, I have a plan,' Frank said, tapping his nose with his index finger. 'You'll see on the day.'

On Friday, the Viking was packed. Every gay person who was on the scene was there to see how Rosie's mother's visit would pan out. 'We'll never be able to carry it off,' said a lanky, skinny, camp queen with a mop of frizzy hair. 'A few drinks in, we'll all forget about trying to be butch and we'll be screaming. So unless his mother is blind, she's going to know she's in a gay bar.'

Frank seemed strangely quiet. I went over to the bar. 'Jaysus, Rosie, you look like you just fell off the cross. Let me check your wrists for holes,' I said dramatically. 'Let's have a drink. It'll steady your nerves for when your ma gets here.' I looked around the bar. Everyone had made the effort, as per Frank's orders. Gay guys and lesbians were pretending they were boyfriend and girlfriend, there was no leather in sight and we could have been in any bar in Dublin. No wonder straight people think there's so few of us, I thought, when we look exactly like everybody else.

'Yeah, let's have a drink,' Frank replied. 'I need one. My mother rang; she's on her way from the bus station.'

Just then the bar door opened and in walked a very elegant woman in her mid-fifties. Frank went pale, bolted his drink and shoved his glass under the vodka optic. He knocked that one back too, and went over to greet his mother. He led her to a table in the corner and when she was settled, he came back to the bar. Gay men immediately put their arms around the shoulders of lesbians and the lesbians put their arms around the waists of the gay men. The performance began.

Lily Cleary came out from the kitchen with a plate of beef, potatoes and veg in his hand. 'Is your mother here yet, Rosie?' he asked. 'Do you want me to bring the food over to her?'

Frank snatched the plate of food from Lily's hand. 'No, what I want you to do is to go down to the cellar and change the Guinness barrel. Here, Rory, you take this over to my mother, introduce yourself and keep her talking. I'll send Mona over with a glass of red wine for her. Introduce Mona as your girlfriend.' Mona was a barmaid on her day off, but she wasn't going to miss this.

I brought the food over to Mrs McCann, put it on the table in front of her and introduced myself. 'Frank's told me so much about you,' I said, giving her a big smile and a firm handshake.

Mrs McCann surveyed the room. 'Isn't this lovely?' she said, smiling at everybody who caught her eye. I introduced Mona as my girlfriend and as we were chatting away, a steady stream of customers, male and female, came over to say hello to Frank's mother and to tell her how wonderful they thought Frank was. Everybody behaved themselves and not one person dropped his or her act for even one moment. And for three to four hours, Mrs McCann was the centre of attention.

My two good friends Derek and Joe were there but they were at opposite ends of the bar shooting each other dagger looks. Uh-oh, they must be fighting, I thought. They had a tempestuous relationship, even though they were devoted to each other. I sidled over to Derek. 'Alright, Debbie? You and Joe not talking? '

'Joe's been misbehaving again,' Derek said, pointing an accusatory finger at Joe. 'He was in the sauna last night. He denies it, but I know he was there.' The sauna was where gay people went to meet other gay people for no-conversations, no-names, no-strings sex.

'Well, if he says he wasn't there, then maybe he wasn't,' I said reasonably.

'Oh, he was there all right,' Derek said, outraged that Joe had been cheating. 'I know he was, because I was in the next cubicle! I got out without him noticing that I was in there as well.'

Frank came over at regular intervals to replenish his mother's drink and to sit and chat for a while. I couldn't believe how well everything was going, but having spoken to Mrs McCann, I had a strong feeling that she couldn't have cared less that her son was gay. But Frank wasn't ready to come out and the people on the scene accepted that and came together to help one of their own. I thought it was fabulous.

Eventually Frank said it was time they left to go to the bus station. Mrs McCann put her coat on and with calls of 'Lovely to see you' and 'You must come again', Frank and his mother set off.

'I'll be back in an hour, Rory,' he said over his shoulder, as he led his mother out of the bar. 'Will you do me a favour and go down to the cellar and bring up a couple of bottles of vodka? The keys are behind the bar.'

That all went well, I thought, as I picked up the keys and went to the cellar. I opened the door and was pushed against the wall by Lily Cleary as he came rushing out. 'Where's Rosie McCann? I'll kill her!' he wailed as he ran up the stairs. 'Jesus, Mary and Joseph, I've been locked in that cellar for hours. Rosie locked me in. Now I know how Anne Boleyn felt when she was locked in the tower.' He waved his hand in front of his face like a fan, rising to the drama of it all. 'Oh God, I need a drink,' he squealed like a schoolgirl, 'I'm as sick as a plane to Lourdes.' So that was Rosie's plan to deal with the Lily problem and hiding him from Mrs McCann. It had worked too.

I had often thought about what it might be like to come out and while I knew that this was something my family weren't ready for, I hoped that my friends would be more accepting.

I used to love going to nightclubs with my great friend Annette Wall, so it was only right and proper that I was sharing an apartment with her when I came out. But my story begins in Suesey Street, one of the nightclubs on Leeson Street, which came alive after normal night spots finished. Those dingy basements would be hopping until dawn and we loved that, because we had just enough time to drive home, have a quick shower and go to work.

It was in Suesey Street that I came to realise that not all straight men were one hundred per cent straight. It was the eighties and people were experimenting. The club had lots of corners that weren't very well lit, and lots of groping in the dark went on. And was I happy? You better believe it. I was young, pretty and single and I was finding out what the world had to offer. And, like me, there were many other young men who were not admitting they were gay and it seemed there were even more again who would claim to be straight, but would go offside if they had a few drinks and if the opportunity presented itself.

I loved dancing and it was easy to manoeuvre your way to someone who caught your eye. The dance floors in these basement clubs were no bigger than postage stamps, so I could do a disco twirl and I'd end up bumping into the guy whose eye I'd caught on the other side of the floor. I'd apologise for bumping into him, he'd say that it was okay and the conversation was up and running. And more often than not, we'd end up in one of the dark corners with a bottle of wine. Afterwards it was usually the same routine. He'd say anxiously, 'I'm not really gay, you know. I like women. You won't tell anyone, will you?' These were basically the unwritten terms of the agreement. A grope was okay but it was to be kept a secret. And who was I going to tell anyway? I wasn't out for a start. So we all kept secrets. We never boasted about conquests, like straight lads did: we just got on with doing what we were doing, having a good time and not really realising how odd our lives were, living in the shadows.

Initially I thought that if I told my straight friends that I was gay, they'd abandon me or make my life a misery, but once I'd made terrific gay friends, like Robert and Ken, I became more confident. If my old friends abandoned me, I reasoned, it wouldn't matter because I'd have gay friends. I wouldn't be left friendless. But when to tell them? You didn't just blurt out, 'I'm gay.' Well, not in 1980s Dublin.

Even most of the people on the gay scene in Dublin at that time weren't out to their friends. So I didn't tell them, I showed them. I didn't plan it, but when I came out, I kicked those closet doors wide open.

Annette and I had yet another party at our place in Milltown and the apartment was rocking. Our old school friends were there and we each had new friends from work and from clubbing. It was a great mix of people. There was one guy there, Maurice, a singer, who myself and Annette knew from the clubs. He used to sing show tunes in restaurants, at charity functions and at weddings. Unfortunately, there was nothing unusual about his voice. He was one of many who could carry a tune. He never got the breaks because of that, but what Maurice had was charm and looks. He had a permanent tan, courtesy of sun beds, which showed off his stunning blue eyes and whiter-than-white teeth. And when he smiled, he could light up a room. And before I go all Mills & Boon here, he was drop-dead gorgeous. I was infatuated with him, but assumed he was straight. He always had a girl hanging off his arm, so to speak. I used to go see him if he was working in a restaurant. I'd have a meal and he'd join me at my table and have a drink when he had a break. We'd talk about everything and anything, including sex. We talked about sex a lot. If he was to be believed, he was having it off with a different girl every night. No wonder I assumed he was straight. I invited him to our party and he accepted. If being good friends was all that was on offer then I was fine with that.

Now, as the party was in full swing, Maurice said, 'You've a lovely apartment. Would you like to give me a tour?' There wasn't much to see: it *was* a lovely two-bedroom apartment, but that was it. Still, I showed him around, eventually taking him out on the balcony to see the night time view. Then, looking me straight in the eye, he said, 'And where's your bedroom?'

With the orchestra going off in my head, I struggled to speak. 'Eh, it's this way,' I stammered, leading him towards my room. Don't be silly Rory, I thought. He's just being polite and wants to see your record collection. (I sometimes have these conversations in my mind. Does that make me mad?) We were in the bedroom now and I switched on the light. I looked at him in stunned silence as he turned and locked the door and then he was all over me like a rash. We were both a bit pissed and there was quite a bit of stumbling and tripping over and giggling as we tried to get undressed.

I wish I could describe what happened as a romantic, stop-the-lights, stars-exploding-in-the-background type of experience, but I can't. We went at each other like alley cats. I ripped half the buttons off my shirt because my hands were shaking so much. And, as we dived under the duvet, there was a loud banging on the door. 'Rory, are you in there?' my old school friend Seán Dawson shouted.

'Yeah, I'm here. I'll be out in a while,' I replied. With that, Maurice and I started laughing.

'He's in the bedroom with somebody,' I could hear Seán saying. 'I could hear them laughing.' With that, it was

Annette's turn to bang on the door, 'Rory Cowan, who have you got in that bedroom?' she asked jokingly, in a voice just like my mother's. 'I won't have that carry-on under my roof.'

Well, I wasn't going to tell her who I was in bed with, so I said, 'It doesn't matter. Enjoy the rest of the party. I'll see you tomorrow.' There was a bit more banter between us from either side of the door and then BOOM: 'Jaysus, he's in bed with a fellah,' somebody shouted. 'He's a bleedin' queer.' I hadn't closed the curtains and I forgot that if you leaned over the side of the balcony, you could see into my bedroom. But somebody calling me a queer? In my own apartment? That was too much. I wasn't having that!

I jumped up out of bed and wrapped the bath towel that I'd had hanging over the radiator around me and stormed into the lounge. 'Which one of you scummy bastards called me a queer?' I demanded angrily. And when there was no reply, I said, 'Right, party's over. Sling your hooks, the lot of you. Get the fuck out of my house.' I was really angry. Angry about being referred to as a queer and angry for letting myself be outed rather than deciding who I was going to tell first. I was shaking with temper.

Then I heard, 'Rory Cowan, I slept with you loads of times and you never laid a finger on me.' I turned to see Seán Dawson standing there, hands on his hips, and with a look of mock outrage on his face. 'What was wrong with me?'

My jaw dropped open and I started to laugh.

'Seriously, what's wrong with me?' he asked, jokingly. 'When your family went to the Isle of Man last year, I slept in the same bed with you for the two weeks and you never made a pass at me.' He was laughing now too.

'And if I did, would it have got me anywhere?' I replied, with a grin on my face.

'It certainly would not,' he said, snorting with laughter, 'but I would have taken it as a compliment if you'd tried.' And then, as if an afterthought, he said, 'Get back into that fella before he falls asleep and we'll continue on with the party.'

'Right!' I said. 'Goodnight.'

The phone in our apartment was on a stand in the hall opposite my bedroom door. Everybody must have wanted to use it and the queue must have stretched into the kitchen because for the next few hours all I could hear was the sound of people pushing buttons and a moment later saying, 'You'll never guess who's queer,' to whoever was on the other end of the phone.

'Gay, not queer,' I'd roar from the bedroom.

'Sorry Rory,' they'd say, before continuing, 'go on, guess. Rory Cowan,' they'd announce. 'He's in bed with a fella now. I swear.' It seemed like my news was not my news anymore, it was everybody else's news. And, come to think of it, I'd never got to tell anybody in the first place.

The next morning, when I wandered into the kitchen, Annette was sitting at the island counter, having a cup of coffee. 'The kettle's boiled if you want a cup,' she said. 'Where's Maurice?'

I shuffled across the kitchen floor, feeling a bit sheepish. 'He's having a shower,' I replied in a small voice.

'Rory, why didn't you tell us before now?' she enquired.

I told her that I'd felt I couldn't say anything previously because of my fear of how people would react, and that I was afraid of losing my friends if they knew I was gay. Annette was looking at me with a quizzical expression on her face and then tears came to her eyes. 'We wouldn't have cared,' she said quietly. 'We'd have been one hundred per cent behind you.' And with that, her voice changed from quiet to dramatic. 'Seán Dawson is telling everybody,' she said, waving her hands around for effect. 'He thinks it's great news. He wants us to meet him and the gang in Sandyford House at lunchtime.'

Meeting the gang that day felt like I was going to be fed to the lions. But after I had my breakfast, had a shower, kissed Maurice at the door and arranged to meet him later that night, myself and Annette took off for Sandyford House. We went in Annette's car. 'I'm going to be drinking,' I told her, as I poured myself a stiff vodka to steady my nerves before we set off.

When we got to the pub it was packed. I walked in with my head down, hoping nobody would notice the flush of red on my face. In the corner was Seán Dawson, his brothers Noel and Pat, his sister Antoinette or Anto as she was known, Johnny and Mark Byrne, all school friends from St Benildus, and a few others. They had obviously heard the gossip and wanted to hear more. Oh Christ, I thought, what have I let myself in for? I got myself and Annette a drink at the bar and then we sat down beside Seán. Nobody seemed to know what to say and everybody looked like they had just discovered something very interesting in the bottom of their glasses. In fact, they were looking anywhere except at each other or at me. Then Seán Dawson stood up. 'Ladies and gentlemen, I have an announcement to make,' he said, his voice booming out like he was the chairman of a social club. 'This is our friend, Rory Cowan, and he's a queer.'

I coughed and spat out a mouthful of drink with the shock of what I was hearing. 'Sorry Rory,' he said, correcting himself, 'he's gay. Now, if anyone in here has a problem with that, would they let me or Noel know and we'll sort it out in the car park later.' With that everybody in our group started clapping and amid lots of congratulations, 'Well done, Rory,' and similar comments, others in the pub started clapping too. I was mortified and delighted at the same time. What on earth had I been worrying about? None of my friends gave a damn that I was gay. On the contrary, they were delighted to have a gay friend. They thought it was the coolest thing.

Seán sat down and said, 'Does your mother know?' When I told him she didn't, he shook his head from side to side and said in a mock sad voice: 'It'll put her in the hospital when I tell her.' And, with that, both of us burst out laughing.

So, that was my coming out – to my friends at least. But, while Frank McCann was a fully-fledged member of the gay scene, I don't think he ever came out to his family and, as far as I know, they never knew he was gay until it was splashed all over the front pages of every national newspaper in Ireland. In 2002 or 2003 Frank met this other gay man in one of Dublin's gay bars. Both were drunk and they had a one-night stand. Within a few hours, Frank had laughed the whole thing off, but the person he'd spent the night with reacted differently. He started stalking Frank. He moved from where he lived to a flat very near to Frank's home. He followed Frank into a bar one night and started snapping photographs of him and wouldn't stop until he was thrown out. Then he started hanging around outside the apartment block where Frank lived and would make hand gestures at him, mimicking a handgun, whenever Frank spotted him.

Frank reported the threats to the police. He was told to keep a record of events and that, if the man attacked Frank in any way, the gardaí would arrest him. On the night of 2 March 2004, Frank rang me to ask if I was going to the karaoke in the Front Lounge that night. The Front Lounge was a gay-friendly bar and Panti Bliss, a fabulous drag queen, hosted karaoke sessions there every Tuesday night. I couldn't go because I was in Manchester, where *Mrs Brown's Boys* was opening a show in the Opera House that night.

Frank had worked in a few gay bars in Manchester and he told me which bars I should go to while I was there. Later that night, many of the cast from *Coronation Street* came to see the show. Keith Duffy from Boyzone, who was a friend of ours, was appearing in *Corrie* at that time and he brought all his cast mates to see our show. I wished Frank had been there to see that because he had been a huge *Corrie* fan since the sixties; he never missed an episode. I'll ring him after the show, I thought. He'll be delighted.

But after the show, I got a call from a friend, Barry Bowes, to say that Frank had been stabbed and was in hospital. He had no other details. I later found out that at about 11.15 p.m., the guy who had been stalking Frank for months had come into the Front Lounge. I don't know whether he was a chef or a trainee chef, but he had a set of knives for the job. He took the second-biggest chef's knife that he had and walked up to Frank, grabbed him by the hair and cut his throat from one side to the other. From what I could gather Frank died immediately but wasn't pronounced dead until later in hospital.

I was numb with shock. In fact, I was numb for months afterwards. I was so grateful that I was touring with *Mrs Brown's Boys* at the time because being on stage and travelling around the UK gave me a sort of holiday from what was happening in real life. It's a strange thing, but while I was on stage I became another character and my real life became a different thing altogether. And for a couple of hours every night I could laugh and enjoy myself, before the darkness came.

I missed Frank's funeral because I was touring. I heard that a group of gay people from Dublin went to Bailieborough for it. They didn't want to draw attention to themselves, so at the graveside they stood at the back of the crowd. After the burial the McCann family got into the mourning cars to be driven home. Mrs McCann stopped the first mourning car, got out and walked over to the groups of gay men and women and hugged them all, saying, 'I believe you were Frank's friends in Dublin. Thank you very much for being his friends.'

In 2005 the man who killed Frank was charged with the crime. He denied the charge. A psychologist testified that the man was suffering from paranoid delusions at the time of the murder, so he was found guilty but insane. He was sentenced to be detained at the Central Mental Hospital in Dublin 'Until the pleasure of the government be known.' In one brief moment Frank's killer did something that shattered my life for quite a while. He murdered one of my best friends, one of the nicest men I knew, in an act of savagery that I've never forgotten.

Life would never be quite the same again.

ELEVEN

Tubthumping

When you're doing panto, there are usually two, sometimes three, shows per day. When the mid-afternoon matinée is finished there's roughly a two-and-a-half-hour break for rest and food before the evening show. The cast don't usually go out for food themselves during the break, because it would mean taking all their make-up off and having to get it all done again for the evening show. Instead, they might get someone to run out for a sandwich or a salad, or ring a local restaurant and ask them to deliver food to the stage door.

However, on this particular afternoon at Christmas 2017, we all decided we'd go to Eddie Rockets, which is two or three doors down from the Olympia. I had an urge for something I hadn't had, or missed, in years: a chicken fillet burger and chips.

We put our normal clothes on, and with our heads down, and in full panto make-up, we ran to the restaurant, hoping nobody would notice us. It turned out Eddie Rockets was packed with people who had either been to the afternoon show or who were going to the evening one. Everyone noticed us and everyone wanted photos with us, which we found hilarious. I'm sure there are many of those odd photos floating about on social media. One woman who took a picture of me said, 'Rory, do you know what I'm going to do with this picture?'

'What? Are you going to get it framed and put it beside your bed?' I asked jokingly.

'Not at all, Rory,' she said with a big grin, showing that she still had all her own teeth. 'It's sleep I want, not nightmares. No, listen,' she said, slapping my forearm, 'I'm going to get this made into a big picture and I'm going to put it on the mantelpiece ... to keep the kids away from the fire.' What a fabulous image. That woman summed up Dublin wit to me.

When our food orders arrived, one of the young dancers reminded me that I had to tell them the story of Brendan O'Carroll hiring me. 'Oh, that,' I said dismissively, 'I can barely remember. Let's talk about something else.' I didn't want to appear too keen and I also wanted to build them up.

'Ah, just tell them, Rory,' said Ryan Andrews, who was playing my son Jack in the panto.

'Oh, well, all right then, if you insist. Picture it. Dublin 1991 ...' I was doing my best impression of Sophia from

The Golden Girls. 'A youngish gay man is unemployed ...'
And I told them the story.

I had been made redundant from EMI Ireland after working
for the company for fourteen years, which I'll get to, but
at that time I'd started dipping my toe into management,
booking acts and promoting shows. I had booked Brendan
for a few shows in pubs around Dublin and all but one were
very successful. The not very successful show was in a venue
long closed, the Wexford Inn on Camden Street. After the
show, Brendan asked me if I had lost money on the gig. I
said I had and he said he wouldn't expect his full fee and
we'd split the takings from the door. We both lost money on
that show, but I know he appreciated the promotion I did
on the successful shows we did together and I appreciated
how hilariously funny he was and how decent he was to
take a drop in his fee.

Shortly after that, Brendan called me to a meeting in a bar
in Dublin with him, his band and his crew. Brendan told me
that he was looking for a publicist and he had two people
in mind for the job, myself and another person, who was
already involved in PR. He was trying to decide which
person was most suitable for the job. And this is where it
got interesting. I made my pitch for the position and told
him what I thought I could bring to his organisation.

As I told my story, I knew the young members of the panto
cast were really interested; they were hanging on my every
word. If I can keep youngsters interested in what I'm saying,
then I should have studied to be a teacher, I thought. The cast

members were all fans of *Mrs Brown's Boys* and here I was, giving them first-hand information about the beginnings of what would become the Mrs Brown phenomenon.

After I made my pitch, Brendan's business partner at the time, Gerry Browne, said he just had one question. I had a feeling what was coming, but I was going to wait to be asked. He was getting flustered, trying to ask his question in a roundabout way, while I just stood there looking at him, saying nothing.

Eventually, Brendan said, 'What he wants to know is if you're gay.'

'Yes,' I said, knowing that I could be talking myself out of a job.

'You've got the job.'

For a moment, I was stunned. 'Are you giving me the job because I'm gay?' I asked, with a hint of confusion in my voice.

'Yeah, I am,' Brendan replied with a big smile on his face. 'I've heard that gay people are very creative, so that's a plus. But you also told us the truth when we asked you the question. We can trust you. That's most important. Welcome on board.'

At this stage, the younger cast members were looking at me in disbelief. 'You got a job because you were gay and other people could lose their jobs because they were gay, only twenty-five years ago?' one of the dancers asked.

'That's how it was back then. Brendan O'Carroll was the exception to the rule. In fact, Brendan did a lot for gay rights back then. We're talking 1991 here. Decriminalisation didn't come into effect until 1993.'

I have to say, I was feeling great being able to tell these kids, some of them gay, what it was like for gay people in Ireland up until the early nineties.

'*Mrs Brown's Boys* started on RTÉ 2FM as a radio soap opera,' I told the kids. 'It started in 1992, when you could be sent to jail if you were convicted of having sex with another man. In most TV shows, gay characters were figures of fun, or had tragic lives,' I explained.

'Hang on,' one of the kids interrupted, 'A man could go to jail for having sex with another man?'

I nodded.

'So, if a man had sex with another man, he could be locked up in a place where there's only men? Not a woman in sight? What were the judges thinking?'

I had to admit he had a point.

'In the radio series, Brendan wrote in two gay characters, Rory and Dino, who were in a relationship. This was a year before gay sex was decriminalised. Brendan broke a taboo,' I said. 'He wrote two gay characters into a prime-time radio show and he made those characters likeable and just the same as anybody else. And I was there when he was doing this. I played Rory on that radio soap opera. I knew something big was happening.'

One young girl, her jaw hanging, said, 'Does that mean you were part of history?'

I laughed and said, 'We're all part of history. Brendan didn't change the law for gay people. He just pushed the envelope. He made people think. And that is how change comes.'

Now it was time to get back to the theatre and prepare for the evening show. 'Right, kids,' I said as we were leaving, 'do you all know the difference between gay and queer?'

One piped up: 'Queer is an insult.'

'That's true. But there are bigger differences. Queer is what you are when your boss fires you because of your sexuality. Gay is what you are, since 1993, when you take him to a tribunal and win. And finally, queer is what you are in Roscommon, where they voted No in the same-sex marriage referendum. Gay is what you are everywhere else in Ireland.'

So that, in a nutshell, is how I began with *Mrs Brown's Boys*. But let's go back to the beginning of the story. It's true that I've been able to spot the turns in my life quickly: my da getting me a job in a record shop run by EMI, which led to a job in a record company and a career in music PR. The next turn was going to see Brendan O'Carroll in a pub in Ranelagh. Little did I know that this complete accident would change my life for ever.

It was 1990 and I was still working for EMI when a friend of mine, the fabulous Carol Hanna, who worked with Louis Walsh and ran her own booking agency, rang and invited me to see an act she was promoting in the Sandford Inn in Ranelagh. I ummed and aahed, thinking that I had no intention of going to see an Irish comedian in action. I wasn't a big fan of that kind of entertainment, the Jury's cabaret thing that was all the rage at the time. While it was good, it wasn't my idea of a night out.

But the gods must have been looking down on me, because another friend, Gary Kavanagh of Peter Mark, rang me and said, 'Rory, Carol invited me to this gig, will you come?' I reluctantly agreed. The comedian was Brendan O'Carroll and he was the funniest comic I'd ever seen. I had the night of my life, howling with laughter at the show, and then I went back to work in EMI and forgot all about it, as you do.

As fate would have it, I was made redundant from EMI the following April, and I wondered what I'd do with myself. I'd spent the past fourteen years promoting Tina Turner and countless other huge acts, but I accepted that a new MD of EMI meant a new broom, no matter how good I was. A new MD usually brought his or her own team on board, and the old team would be gone. I was out, even though I'd loved every minute of it. That's the way it was in the music business in those days.

I can still remember one of my last projects for EMI. My da would give me a lift to work sometimes and we'd hear Father Brian D'Arcy on 2FM, playing clips of recordings of the kids at Rutland Street School retelling Bible stories in their own inimitable way. We'd roar with laughter at these retellings and I thought it would be brilliant if it was released commercially, so I approached Father Brian D'Arcy, who agreed to release *Give Up Yer Aul Sins* as a cassette tape. He took nothing from it and all profits went to charity.

It took off like a rocket. People were buying dozens of tapes at a time for friends and family at home and abroad and the shops couldn't keep it in stock. This humble little cassette went double platinum, even though the teacher who had first recorded the children was now elderly and suffering from dementia. *Give Up Yer Aul Sins* went on to become an animated film, which was nominated for an Oscar. I'm proud of the fact that releasing these stories was my idea. It didn't save me from redundancy, but it's a fond memory.

A less fond memory from this period was when I almost did time in jail. And it was my own fault. When I was working in EMI I had a company car, with insurance, petrol and upkeep of the car all paid for by the company. The one thing it wouldn't pay was parking fines. But, being young and disrespectful of the law, I used to park my car as close as I could to wherever I wanted to go. As a result, I accumulated a number of fines and because I didn't pay them, additional penalties were added. It got to the stage where I owed £1,250 in fines. And this was 1991, so that would probably be thousands of euros today. In the midst of all this I was made redundant. One afternoon there was a knock on my door. Two gardaí were standing there.

'Hello, Mr Cowan, we've a warrant here for your arrest in relation to unpaid parking fines.'

'You what?!' I replied, thinking there must be some mistake. A warrant for my arrest?

The garda nodded. 'There are a number of outstanding parking fines and unless you can pay twelve hundred and fifty pounds now, you're going to jail for fifteen days.'

I started to panic. I didn't have that amount of cash and there was no way I could find it. 'Can I call my solicitor first?' I pleaded.

When I got permission, I rang my solicitor. 'Listen,' I said anxiously, 'you won't believe this, but there's two policemen at the door with a warrant for my arrest. Fifteen days in jail!' I filled him in on all the details, becoming increasingly distressed, and ending with, 'What'll I do?'

He told me to calm down and instructed me: 'Tell the guards you are going to petition the Minister for Justice.'

'That's grand, Rory,' one of the guards said. 'We'll wait until we hear from her. Have a good evening'. And off they went.

'What the hell is petitioning the Minister for Justice?' I said to my solicitor, delighted with the turn of events.

'Okay, Rory, here's what you have to do to get the fines written off or reduced. You write a letter to the minister, telling her about your outstanding fines. Say you are unable to pay because you were made redundant and you're behind on your mortgage. Say you have final demands for your gas and electric bills.'

I didn't know what to think. After being made redundant, it was certainly true that I couldn't find £1,250, whatever about gas bills and the leccy.

'You have to plead poverty,' my solicitor said. 'You have to show that in your current circumstances you just can't afford to pay the fines.'

I can't, I thought miserably. 'And will that work?' I said doubtfully.

'Yep! It'll work.'

That night, I wrote the most heartfelt letter I could manage. I wrote everything my solicitor had told me to and while I might not have been in quite the dire straits I claimed, things were certainly pretty tight. That £1,250 could be the difference between paying my mortgage and not paying it the following month.

A couple of weeks later, I got a lovely reply from the Minister for Justice. She said that she was very sorry to hear about my unfortunate circumstances and she hoped the situation I found myself in would improve. She said she would reduce the fines to £300 and gave me six months to pay. At the end of the letter, she warned me that if the fines weren't paid, they would revert to the full amount. I was delighted and relieved. I filed the letter away and promptly forgot about it.

Six months and a day later, there was a knock on my door at seven o'clock in the morning. I dragged myself out of bed and when I opened the door it was the same two gardaí who'd visited me just over six months before. 'Rory, it's those unpaid fines again. If you can't give us twelve hundred and fifty pounds, you've got to do fifteen days in jail.'

'Hang on, it's not twelve hundred and fifty, it's only three hundred pounds.' It was then I remembered the sting in the tail in the minister's letter. 'Would you mind calling back this afternoon so I can make arrangements to get the money to pay the fines?' I asked sheepishly.

The two gardaí looked at each other and started to laugh. 'Rory,' the younger one said, 'I don't think you understand. We don't make appointments. You have to come with us now. You're under arrest and we've to take you to Mountjoy. Now get dressed and come on.'

There was nothing I could do at seven in the morning. I'd have to go to jail and, hopefully, when I got there, I could make a phone call to my solicitor when his office opened. 'You wouldn't mind driving around the corner and waiting until I have a shower, would you?' I asked earnestly. 'I don't want my neighbours to see me getting into a police car.'

They agreed to do that but warned me, 'You've got half an hour. Don't make us come back.'

How I stood up in the shower, I don't know. My legs were like jelly. Only a couple of years ago I was having dinner with the likes of Tina Turner and Cliff Richard, and now I was being sent to jail for unpaid parking fines. Oh, calamity! And I'd brought it all on myself. I finished my shower, got dressed, locked up the house and went to meet the gardaí around the corner. If anybody asked where I was when I got back, I'd have to tell them I'd gone on a fortnight's holiday.

I was shaking getting into the car and all the colour had drained from my face. I could see my reflection in the rear-view mirror and I looked like a ghost. Taking people to jail was nothing new to the two gardaí who were escorting me there, but going to prison was a very new thing to me and I didn't like the idea of it one bit.

'Don't worry,' the older guard said, when he noticed my distress, 'You might not have to do your sentence in Mountjoy. Tell the governor you want to go to an open prison.'

It's just as well that I was sitting down because I'd have collapsed if I had been standing. I didn't want to go to any prison, open or closed. I wanted my solicitor to pay the fines at ten o'clock, get me out of prison, and I'd pay him back after I'd somehow got the money together. The rest of the journey was conducted in silence. I sat in the back of the car not believing what was happening. Then a thought came to me and I started to panic. What if there was somebody there that I knew or who recognised me? I'd never to be able to keep this a secret. I'd be known as a jailbird.

The thought didn't have long to fester because we arrived at the jail. I was taken inside through a door beside the big gate. I could hardly breathe. This place looked bleak. Oh, please God, don't let me have to stay here one moment more than necessary, I thought.

The two police escorts handed over the warrant and left and I was led into a side room, where prisoners on their way to court were held until the prison vans came to collect them, or where prisoners who had been convicted were held after being brought from court to jail.

I asked if I could ring my solicitor at ten o'clock. 'You'll have to wait until you see the governor,' he said kindly. He obviously knew this was my first time in jail. I started to relax. I'm not being put in a cell, so that's okay, I thought. I'll just wait here until I see the governor and then I can go home after my solicitor gets me out.

So much for waiting to make a phone call. The governor must have been busy that day. Prisoners were shown into the room I was in. They were chatting away as if this was a normal environment to be in. They were telling each other what they were being charged with. One lad said he was up for stabbing his girlfriend twenty-seven times with a screwdriver. Another was being charged with attempted murder. There were a few 'jump-overs', which I later found out was jumping over a counter of a shop or post office or bank, armed with a weapon, and demanding the person behind the counter hand over all the money in the cash register or safe. At this point, I thought I was going to puke.

Then one young man in his early twenties, who was being charged with double murder, looked at me suspiciously and said, 'What are you in for?'

'Parking fines,' I said meekly. It was as if I had told the funniest joke in the world. They were laughing so much, one of the warders came in to see what was going on. I wished I could see the funny side of it.

When the prison vans arrived, the other prisoners were led out. I was on my own again. Another prison warder came in and asked if I'd like a cup of tea. 'I'd like to see the governor,' I replied. He gave me a cup of tea while I was waiting. I got four cups of tea before I was summoned to meet the governor. It was now two o'clock in the afternoon. I hoped my solicitor would be able to find the money to get me out of here, otherwise I'd be spending at least one night here. I was led into the governor's office. John Lonergan was sitting behind his desk. I was just about to tell him that I could pay the fines, if he would let me make a phone call, when I noticed he had copies of my letter to the Minister for Justice pleading poverty and her reply to me.

'Rory,' he said. 'Are things still as bad as they were six months ago?'

For a split second I wondered what I was going to say. I'd never felt so low in my whole life. I wasn't quite at the poorhouse yet, but I wasn't far off. Why on earth hadn't I paid the fines when I had the money?

The governor said, 'This is no place for you, Mr Cowan.'

Oh, please don't send me to an open prison down the country, I thought.

'You've served your sentence,' he said. And with that he stamped a form.

I couldn't believe what I was hearing. 'Are you serious? I asked in amazement. 'What about the parking fines?'

'Your sentence is completed. You don't have to pay the fines.'

I left the jail at half past two. I'd been there since eight o'clock that morning. In that six and a half hours, my parking fine debt of £1,250 had vanished. I couldn't believe how things had panned out. It was a sign that from now, on, things would get better. It was also a sign that I should pay my parking fines! Everyone has a low point in their lives, and this was certainly one of mine. I felt ashamed and foolish – and I've never done it again.

The following Sunday I went up to my mother's for dinner and when she asked me if I had any news I said that nothing interesting had happened that week. Well; what she doesn't know can't hurt her, I thought.

After being made redundant, I'd dipped my toe in the waters of management, looking after Christy Dignam, who was on hiatus from Aslan, and Conor Gough, in an act called Dignam and Gough. I also managed Mr Pussy, Alan Almsby, a very popular drag act at the time. I learned a lot with Alan. Thanks to my time in EMI, I knew about margins, so when Alan said he'd work as Mr Pussy for £150, I said, 'Alan, with my commission, that's nothing.' So I asked for £500 and the commission was worth me making the calls. And I got it. I'd been used to dealing with big acts, where money wasn't an issue and they never had to haggle! And if anyone chanced their arm, saying something like, 'Can you do anything about the money? It wasn't a great night,' I would shake my head and say, 'Not a penny more, not a penny less.'

When I'd secured Alan's fee, I'd go into him in the dressing room. He'd be sitting there, make-up on, about to put on his wig. 'Have you got the handbag, dear?'

'Yes, I've got the handbag,' I'd say, waving the money at him, whereupon he'd pick up his microphone and bound on stage with a 'Hello, everybody!'

I put the two acts into different venues all over the place and things were going just fine: they were both selling out the gigs. In fact, the owner of a Finglas pub called the Bottom of the Hill, a good cabaret venue, came up to me and said that the two acts that had done best for him were the two I'd put in. And the reason for that was because of my experience at EMI – I wasn't happy just putting a poster in the pub to announce the act. I'd promote big – I'd have posters everywhere and I'd put ads in newspapers. My acts were visible – that was how I worked.

Anyway, this man said to me, 'Is there anyone you could put in for me?

I had a think and then I said, 'Well, there's a comedian I saw about six or seven months ago. If I can find him, he might be good. I'll see if I can get him.'

After a bit of hunting around, I eventually found Gerry Browne, Brendan's manager at the time, and booked him. Brendan's fee was £400. I could work with that, I thought. It was £3 on the door and I made £1,400 on the night. I gave Brendan his £400 and I had £1,000 left over. I thought, that's a bit much, seeing as he's doing all the work, but that's the business.

I started booking him for other venues and it was going very well and Brendan liked the way I was doing things. At the time, he lived in Ashbourne and every time he drove to meetings in town, he'd see posters for the acts I was promoting along the way. This guy knows what he's doing, he thought. Then, one night, I booked him into the Wexford Inn, as I told the cast of the panto, and I lost money – before Brendan made me his first gay publicist!

This was the first glimpse I really had of Brendan in action and the way his mind worked. He didn't really need a publicist, but he liked the way I did things and he saw an opportunity. And the job worked very well, because Brendan was very funny and I was good at my job. After EMI, I'd gone back to college to study for a Higher Diploma in marketing and PR, so I had the piece of paper, and I was always looking for an angle. I also knew everybody in the radio stations and the entertainment journalists. They'd take my calls and agree to write a story on Brendan. I was even able to get Brendan as a clue on the *Star* jumbo crossword on a Saturday.

'Listen, Brendan loves the crossword – any chance you'd put him in as a clue?'

'Ah, yeah,' the journalist replied. 'What does he do?'

'He's a comedian,' I explained.

The next Saturday, there was a picture of Brendan in the middle of the crossword!

The next step came from an old friend on 2FM, DJ Gareth O'Callaghan. I'd called him, telling him that I needed to get Brendan a profile in the media, and he suggested a slot they had called 'What's in the Papers?' where he'd get a celebrity in to read and chat about stories in the papers. I agreed and off Brendan went to 2FM. Now, the stories that Gareth had picked out weren't all that funny, so Brendan decided to embellish them, going off on wild flights of fancy. 'The body of a woman has been found in the Kilkenny Mountains. She's been dead for 510 years. The gardaí are looking for a 530-year-old man to help with their enquiries.' That was one of them, I remember, and another, 'The wind was so bad in Castlebar that a woman rang into say her hen had laid the same egg three times.' They were very funny and Gareth loved them.

After the show, we were having a coffee in the RTÉ canteen and Gareth mentioned that he'd like something new for the show. Brendan said, 'Well, I'm writing a radio soap opera.'

I thought, Are you? You never told me.

'What's it called?' Gareth asked.

'*Mrs Brown's Boys* – about a Dublin widow and her children,' Brendan said confidently. Little did I know what it would go on to be, but as we were leaving, I said to Brendan, 'I didn't know you were writing a radio soap opera.'

'I am now,' he said. He'd jumped at the opportunity, which

he was brilliant at doing. So we recorded ten episodes of three or four minutes each and Mrs Brown very quickly became huge on the radio. We heard that prisoners in Mountjoy were asking to change their exercise times so they could be inside to hear it; taxi drivers outside the Gresham wouldn't pick up fares while it was on. What's interesting about the radio soap is that it was an early example of Brendan's style of working. He couldn't afford to pay actors, so the cast were all amateurs, which he liked, because it was more flexible. You can't get professionals for a long period of time – after two weeks, they aren't available, so that's why he never hired 'real' actors, apart from Susie Blake, who played Mrs Nicholson in the TV series, but she didn't go on the road because she wasn't free.

The other reason Brendan liked to use amateurs is that we would follow his directions to the letter. I wasn't at all sure about Rory, the character he created who was, coincidentally, gay. In fact, I begged him not to call him Rory, but Brendan wouldn't budge. 'Call me something stereotypically gay, like Cecil or Nigel,' I said. I'm delighted now, but I wasn't at the time!

We didn't get paid for the soap, because 2FM had no budget for radio drama, so they used to pay us in T-shirts, which we'd sell at gigs. It's not as bad as it sounds – we were linked to a national broadcaster and you can't pay for that kind of publicity. And that's how I was able to get Brendan on *The Late Late Show*. As he was an unknown quantity at the time, it took them a long time to agree, but when they did – well, the rest is history.

Gay Byrne, who hosted the show then, was brilliant with him. The previous guests had run short, so Brendan had thirty-five minutes to fill, instead of the usual fifteen, but Gaybo only asked him a total of four questions in all that time. Brendan did all the talking! I can still remember the opener: 'Brendan. Your mother.' As I've said, Brendan's mother was the Labour TD Maureen O'Carroll, and she was a legend in Dublin because of the work she did with domestic-abuse survivors and the poor. With those three words, Brendan was off. Unlike some, Gay Byrne was brilliant at open-ended questions that couldn't be answered with a yes or no. He simply let Brendan be himself and it was magic.

The *Late Late* opened up the whole country to us. The week before, I'd been ringing venues trying to book new gigs and I was struggling, but now everyone wanted Brendan. For example, before the *Late Late*, I rang a certain Dublin pub and said to the owner that I was looking for a show for Brendan for Friday night, any Friday night. I told him that I could take a guarantee of £500 or the door, a good deal.

'Brendan O'Carroll – I wouldn't have him cleaning the car park,' this man said. 'He's a filthy swine.' Some people didn't like Brendan's use of bad language. There's nowhere you can go from that, so I put down the phone and moved on to the next venue. Three days later, Brendan was on the *Late Late* and the next day the owner rang me. 'I've been thinking about Brendan O'Carroll. I might have a Friday available …'

'The deal's changed,' I said. 'I want one Friday every month for four months, £3,000 per show, guaranteed.' I got it!

For a year after the *Late Late*, we gigged for 300 nights out of 365. When I hear bands nowadays saying they did six shows and they were exhausted after it, I think Oh, please – that's a rehearsal. We covered the whole country: Ballina one night, then Cork, then Belfast, over three nights – and we were coming home to Dublin every night. Now, when I drive through Ireland, I spot all the places we gigged in and it brings back a lot of happy memories.

I think we all enjoyed ourselves because the whole business was new to us. For example, we never entertained the idea of 'luck' money – the practice, common at the time, of paying back the venue a portion of the take at the door. Dermot 'Bugsy' O'Neill, who plays Granddad now, was a roadie at the time, humping the gear in and out of pubs and clubs and collecting money at the door. He was a tough guy, and then he was only in his thirties, so when an owner said they weren't paying us because the place wasn't full, even though you could hardly move, Brendan would say, 'That's no problem. We'll take it in kind. Bugsy, take the television.'

Dermot would go up to the TV and pretend to unscrew it from the wall and the owner would say, 'Ah, here's your bleeding money, you'll never play here again.' And they'd ring the next day looking to book more shows!

We travelled in an eight-seater van that Brendan had, and another van with Pat 'Pepsi' Shields, who would go on to play Mark Brown in the TV show, and Bugsy and the gear in it. We'd stop off and have coffee along the way and it was very sociable and pleasant. We weren't like some of the showbands, many of whom became alcoholics because they'd be sitting around in venues having a few drinks. We were like army buddies, and everything was brilliant.

One night we were in Sligo and because we were playing somewhere close the next night, there was no point going home, so we booked into a hotel. We all shared rooms, and I was with Dermot. This night, I ended up picking up a guy up in a bar in Sligo and taking him back to my room. Now, Bugsy could snore for Ireland, so I told the guy, 'If Bugsy's snoring, it's all right, but if he stops, he's woken up.' Into the bed we get and Bugsy is snoring away, and then he stops – and we freeze. He lets out a loud snore and we know he's fallen back to sleep.

The next morning, Bugsy woke up and got out of bed, and as he headed off to the bathroom, he caught sight of the two of us in the bed. He took one look at my friend and let a roar out of him. 'Get him out! If he's still here when I come out of the shower, he's going out through the window.' I knew that Bugsy was only joking, but still, I hustled my friend out of the room.

'You won't believe it,' Bugsy told everyone later, 'He was in bed with another fella!'

This was all new to them. None of them knew much about the gay scene, but they were keen to find out. I remember bringing them to the George bar on South Great George's Street in Dublin one night. They'd never been to a gay bar and they were expecting a big thrill. I could see the disappointment on their faces when they saw the place. It was just a bar. I don't know what they were expecting, but Bugsy wouldn't go to the toilet 'in case one of them comes near me'.

I said, 'Bugsy, they're gay, they're not blind.'

Then two guys came in wearing fur coats and make-up. They weren't in drag, but it was the done thing to dress up a bit for this place, and they sat behind Bugsy, sipping away on their pints through a straw, so not to ruin their lipstick. Bugsy turned around to see the two men drinking Guinness through a straw. 'What the fuck are you?' he said. We thought it was hilarious. Now, in case you think otherwise, Bugsy was the nicest, sweetest guy and, at the slightest sign of trouble, he'd be there.

Sometimes, at gigs, I'd walk into the crowd to sell programmes and T-shirts and I'd get a bit of abuse. 'Get away, you bleedin' queer.' That kind of thing. I'd call Bugsy over. 'Are you all right?' he'd say, in a certain way, and they'd quickly change their tune.

Brendan and the gang accepted me as gay; they'd give me an unbelievable slagging, but it was quite the opposite of prejudice, and having a gay member of the team gave them a bit of kudos – 'We've a gay person working for us,' they'd boast.

By the time we'd been gigging around the country for about five years, doing 250–300 gigs a year, Brendan decided he'd had enough. In our fourth year on the road, he had noticed that crowds were down and that the pubs were busy but not packed. He saw very quickly that he had to change direction, so he decided to write a new stage play and he'd cast everyone from the team.

The result was *The Course*, which was about a group of no-hopers who have to pass an exam to sell life assurance door to door. It was actually based on a course that Brendan had done years before. He played Joe Daly, the course co-ordinator, who passed everybody, and other members of the group included an alcoholic, a housewife, a prostitute, a wannabe actor and an eejit, for want of a better word. That's where the fun started, with Brendan teaching the worst class ever.

The Dublin Theatre Festival wanted a big name and this was Brendan's first play, but the arrangement for the play to be part of the festival didn't work out and we ended up being booked into the Tivoli Theatre on Francis Street for a month, with debts of £100,000, a huge sum at the time. You could have bought two houses with it. Thank God, *The Course* outgrossed everything that year, so the following year we booked it into the Gaiety Theatre, a much bigger venue.

Brendan then wrote *Grandad's Sure Lilly's Still Alive*, set in an old folks' home. The play was written just before the scandals about the abuse of elderly people in residential homes. The title came from something one of the characters said when called upon to 'sort out' a character who was a virgin. Lilly was a prostitute he'd known years before. Off they go in search of Lilly, but find her daughter instead, and the brothel is now a cabaret lounge. In the end, the home gets closed down and the evil matron gets her just desserts. I thought it was a terrific play, but for some reason it didn't do as well as we'd hoped. It just didn't click with audiences, which goes to show, you can never tell what will work in this business.

Then Brendan decided to do a movie, a bold move in those days. He paid for it all himself, and the costs were enormous, but it didn't get released and Brendan lost all his money. He's spoken about this himself many times, and about the struggle to repay his debts, but he did it in the end. Nonetheless, it was a real blow to us all. We were all depressed and we had no idea where to go next.

At the time, I was producing radio talk shows, such as Chris Barry on night-time radio. I was very good at it, thankfully and for this confidence, I have to thank my mother. My attitude has always been, 'I can do that,' even if I can't. But Dad was actually the biggest help on the show. We'd have debates every night about topical things and I'd get Dad to call in and be devil's advocate. Dad was a quiet man normally, but he loved the chance to act up, saying things like, 'I hate children. Hate them. My wife wants them, but I wouldn't have them.' He'd just do whatever I asked! I'd also get friends on and prod them to say outrageous things. We did not want to hear, 'I can see both sides of the story.' A friend of mine, who was gay, once rang up – 'Gay Pride? I'd burn the lot of them. I could be here with my kids, seeing them walking down the street in women's clothes.' It caused an uproar.

At the same time as my working life was in flux, I noticed that I was getting very tired and that my eyesight was fading. I also developed a droop on the left side of my face, which I put down to Bell's palsy, a harmless condition. If I'd waited, God knows what might have happened, but I went to the doctor. He told me that I'd had a mild stroke and that was a right kick in the balls. I had no idea what to do next. I went to hospital for tests – questions about who the taoiseach was and what day of the week it was. I thought they were pretty obvious, but I was told I got a few of them wrong and it was then that they knew I definitely had an issue.

After two days, I got the results. I hadn't had a stroke, but I did have a brain tumour. I couldn't take it in. I was only thirty-four – surely I was too young to get sick? And how on earth am I going to tell my mother? I wondered, while I waited in Beaumont A&E for a bed. They were due to operate on me the following morning, so I knew that I had to come up with something.

In the end, I rang her and told her it was something very minor so she wouldn't worry and get Da to drive to the hospital at the speed of light. It didn't stop her, though – she was at my bedside half an hour later. Now I had to tell her the truth.

'Ma,' I said, 'I have a brain tumour.'

She gripped my arm and said, 'Are you telling me everything?'

'For God's sake, Ma, I'm telling you I have a brain tumour, isn't that enough?' I said.

Like all mothers, mine would worry. She was like the Mother of Sorrows and I'd feel worse, not better, after talking to her. I know she didn't mean it, but she just couldn't help herself.

You might not believe it but my main concern, even though I was about to operated on for a brain tumour, was hiding the tattoo I'd had done a few years previously from Ma. My only excuse for this lapse in judgement was that I was drunk. It was a horrible design I'd picked from an image on the wall of the tattoo parlour, a picture of a warrior with a sword held upright, dripping blood.

Anyway, the surgeon came to visit me the day before the operation. He started to tell me what the surgery entailed, but when he got to the part where he said, 'We will drill a small hole in the head,' I stopped him with my best cut-it-out hand sign, kinda like Diana Ross and the Supremes singing, 'Stop in the Name of Love'.

'Doctor, will you know what you're doing when you operate on me?' I asked.

'Yes,' he said, sounding a bit confused about where this conversation was going.

'That's fine then. I don't need to know anything about the operation. I trust you!' I said, perking up.

He was still confused. 'Mr Cowan, people having surgery like to have the procedure explained to them. They want to know the risks,' he said.

'Well, I don't,' I said, sounding more bored than I meant to be. 'Doctor, there's nothing I can do about the procedure. That's your job. If I don't know the risks, I don't worry about the risks. If you do your job properly, I'll be fine.'

The doctor raised a quizzical eyebrow at that and replied, 'Okay, Mr Cowan, I'll make you well.' I was happy with that. Being told I was going to be made well did me more good than being told about drilling into my head.

So the operation was carried out the next day and it was successful and eventually I did get well, as the doctor had promised. How my mother reacted was a different story altogether. She'd been waiting anxiously in the hospital while I was having the surgery. She was there beside my bed when I was coming back to the ward after my operation. I was still a bit woozy from the anaesthetic but when the hospital assistants were moving me from the trolley to the bed, I heard my mother shriek, 'When did you get that tattoo?'

I thought it best to pretend to be asleep until she calmed down!

Just after my mother discovered I had a tattoo, my two friends Frank McCann and Barry Bowes came to visit me in hospital. They picked their moment and arrived up after visiting hours, when they knew I'd be having a nap. I was still groggy from the surgery and I was sleeping a lot, so I didn't even open my eyes to see them standing by my bed. 'Here Rory, sign this,' I could hear Barry say urgently.

'You don't need to read it, just sign it,' Frank's voice added sweetly.

I knew they were up to something, so I opened my eyes and sat up. What they wanted me to sign was a handwritten note on a sheet of paper with the headline, *LAST WILL AND TESTAMENT OF RORY COWAN*. And they had gone on to write that I was leaving everything I owned to them. I began to chuckle as I was reading it and when I looked at them, they had huge big grins on their faces. 'Just in case you're going to die,' Barry snickered.

'Get lost,' I retorted in mock outrage, even though I was delighted to see them. Barry Bowes was a good friend. Straight and married with three children, he was built like a brick shithouse and looked like he should be helping the gardaí with their enquiries. But he had a heart of gold and he would sooner do anybody a good turn rather than a bad one.

'How are you feeling?' he asked me now.

'Rotten,' I replied, wincing. 'Every time I look in the mirror I see a tired, haggard old woman.'

'Well, at least there's nothing wrong with your eyesight,' he responded and the three of us cracked up. It made me think that jokes, even jokes about death, when someone has just had surgery, can be therapeutic. For the first time since I was admitted to hospital, I was in great form.

'Here, you won't believe what they're calling you in the Dragon,' Frank blurted out. The Dragon was one of the main gay bars in Dublin, just up the road from its sister gay bar, the George. Dublin's gay scene revolved around the George and Dragon.

'What are they calling me?' I asked snappily.

'Tammy Tumours,' he exclaimed, laughing heartily. 'Well, I thought it would be a good camp name for you and it seems to have caught on.'

I tried to look cross at the ignominy of being called Tammy Tumours, but that's a hard look to carry off when I was clutching my sides and gasping with laughter. That's typical of the gay scene though. Even something as serious as having a brain tumour is joked about in gossip. While the three of us were convulsed with laughter, we were interrupted by a nurse who had come in to take my blood pressure and temperature. That brought the visit to an end. As the two lads were leaving and as the nurse was taking out the thermometer, Frank said, 'Now, Tammy, open up and say moo.' And with that, they were gone, leaving me gabbling away at the nurse, trying to make excuses for my very odd friends. I don't know what I'd have done without them. The doctor was right – he did make me well, thank God. The tumour wasn't cancerous, so that was an unbelievable relief. I was only out of action for a few weeks.

I'm convinced that I have guardian angels. I can just see them, sitting on a fluffy cloud, dealing cards and smoking and then saying, 'Deal me out, this poor sod needs attention.' I feel incredibly lucky to have survived.

While I was recuperating, Brendan was in a bit of a slump. He had nothing in the pipeline and he didn't want to go back to stand-up, because it would be like starting at the beginning again. He had no plays up his sleeve, either, because he'd focused on the movie. Then Denis Desmond of MCD approached him. A show had been pulled from the Gaiety and he needed something in its place.

'Denis, I have no shows. I don't even feel funny,' Brendan told him.

'Ah, could you not just scribble up something about that aul wan you used to have on the radio?' Denis said.

Brendan thought, I wonder if that would work, and the result was *Mrs Brown's Last Wedding* in 1997–8. Denis put the money up for the production and Brendan supplied the cast and crew and then the money started rolling in. We had a six-week run in the Gaiety Theatre, six shows a week, six days a week, and the play was a phenomenon. We took it all over the country on tour, then back to the Gaiety. By that stage, we'd taken it as far as it could go in Ireland. It became clear to us that either Brendan needed to write another play, or we needed to get out of town, so to speak. So we booked a three-week run in the Pavilion Theatre in Glasgow.

No one else ever worked it that way. Normally, you'd take a week, then extend the run if you got lucky, but we weren't going into a theatre unless we could get three weeks to establish ourselves. The way we looked at it was: the first week we'd lose out, because no one would know we were there; the second week, we might break even, because word would have got out; then in the third week we'd make our money, because word of mouth would have got out and the crowds would have started to come. That was our formula for success.

Now, we could only get private theatres – theatres owned by groups wouldn't take us. And even when we booked the Pavilion in Glasgow, the owner panicked in the first week and said that we'd have to pull the final two weeks, because only £3,000 had been taken at the box office and there were barely any ticket sales.

Brendan said, 'Look, just let the word of mouth get out there.'

We opened that night, and the next night the owner had to take on seven new staff to cope with the demand.

Now we had Glasgow; and on the strength of our success, I went to a theatre in Liverpool and asked for a three-week run, saying that the play had been a huge success in Glasgow. They agreed and the play took off like a rocket. They even had police on horseback for crowd control. So now our annual schedule was booked for most of the year, apart from the school holidays, which Brendan would take off to look after his children.

On the strength of that first play, Brendan wrote a second, *Good Mourning Mrs Brown*, and two years later he wrote a third. He was casting around for an idea and I'd been reading a book about the comedian Dick Emery in which he talks about having an old codger living with his daughter and her husband, and the hook for the sketch was that one day he heard his daughter and son-in-law saying, 'We'll have to get rid of him. Is there a home we could put him into?' The poor man nearly died, but they were talking about the budgie. The germ of the idea was born and it would become the third Mrs Brown play. We ended up doing five Mrs Brown plays and were on the way to a sixth when we were commissioned by the BBC, which was our breakthrough. Before that, we had played from Birmingham north with great success, but south of Birmingham we'd died!

That all changed once we were on the BBC. The next few years would pass in a whirlwind as we toured the five plays and recorded the show and took the plays out on huge stadium tours.

Then there was *Mrs Brown's Boys D'Movie* in 2014. The reviews might have been patchy, but there was no arguing with the box office receipts. The movie made a total of $28.8 million worldwide: not bad for a film with a budget of £3.6 million – tiny by today's standards. It was the top-grossing film in Ireland and opened at number one in the UK.

I didn't have much to do in the film, deliberately, because I was well aware that camp in big doses can be very boring, so I'd said to Brendan, 'Just in and out, Brendan, that's all.' However, I knew that when Rory came on, in the TV show or on stage, something would always happen. He was a foil for Mrs Brown, so when Brendan wrote a scene in the movie where I was to wear a mankini, I could imagine that it would get a big laugh. That doesn't mean that I was keen to do it! It had already been done by the hilarious Borat, Sacha Baron-Cohen's character, and I didn't want to look as if we were copying him. Besides, I was in my fifties at that stage – long past the time to be seen in public in a mankini! However, once I thought about it, I realised that it could be the biggest scene in the movie, so I said, 'Okay, Brendan, I'll do it.' I may not have preserved my dignity, but I stole the show …

The idea was that I would swim the Channel in my mankini to try and raise money for Mrs Brown to buy her market stall from the Russian thugs who now owned it. All I had to do was to jump in, say 'It's freezing,' then jump back out again. Little did I know, they were to cover me in goose fat and put a giant flowery rubber swim hat on me! We filmed the scene on Dollymount Strand, and people walking their dogs on the beach would spot me and yell, 'Hi, Rory!' It wasn't very dignified, but it was funny.

People often ask me if our success was a happy accident, but I've always felt that while luck plays a part, the harder you work, the luckier you get. There was no doubting the fact that everyone loved Agnes Brown. Lots of people thought she was a real woman and they'd bring her flowers and chocolate to the stage door after a show. If Brendan didn't appear, they'd ask where Mrs Brown was, and we'd have to make up an excuse that she was tired and had gone home for a nice lie-down. Someone even got our faces tattooed on his back!

I don't feel lucky, but good timing has certainly played a part in my life. If Da hadn't got me a job in the record shop, I would never have been standing there at the counter when the MD walked by. When the company saw how hard I worked, they gave me the stock-control job, then the stock-control manager left and they gave me his job. So I was doing two jobs. Da, who was still the union rep for EMI, told me, 'Rory, you can't be doing two jobs.' When jobs were thin on the ground, and the rule was 'one man (or woman), one job', I was taking someone's opportunity away from them – that was his reasoning. But I said, 'Da, let me do it. I want to.' He had to say to others in the trade union, 'If he says he can do it, he can do it!'

The next bit of lucky timing came when EMI's sales and marketing manager left to take over BMG records, so they offered me the position, at twenty-four years of age. And even though my redundancy set me back, ultimately I found a new direction. Going to see Brendan O'Carroll at the Sandford Inn all those years ago was definitely good timing, as was being there when the original Rory Brown left.

Fans often say to me, 'Rory, you're very lucky,' and I agree that I was, but I've worked hard too. As has Brendan. The reason Mrs Brown is such a huge hit is because of his unbelievable hard graft as a writer and comic, but it's also down to teamwork.

Things never work out as you expect them to, but that can be a good thing!

TWELVE

Don't Rain on My Parade

Before she developed dementia, the only person Ma didn't mind using bad language was Brendan O'Carroll. She thought he was hilarious and he had this knack of saying potentially offensive things, or swearing, that didn't offend people. Quite the contrary – they used to roar laughing when he did.

When I was in *Mrs Brown's Boys,* we used to go out after the show to meet fans who wanted autographs and photos with the cast. Most nights there would be hundreds of people waiting to meet us. One night, there was a man in a wheelchair halfway down the queue. He was waiting to meet Brendan. Now, every one of the cast could get out to the signings quicker than Brendan. We only had to remove our costumes and our make-up, put on our street clothes and off we'd go to meet the fans. Brendan, on the other hand, had to take off his wig, remove the mole stuck to his face and take off the body suit he wore to get the Agnes Brown shape. And because of the body suit, he used to sweat buckets on stage, so he'd have to have a shower after every performance. By the time he got out to meet the fans, the rest of us were nearly finished.

'Brendan, over here!' the guy in the wheelchair called out.

Brendan replied, 'I'll be with you in a minute. I've to say hello to these people ahead of you. I see you've brought your own seat.'

Everybody in the line laughed, no one more loudly than the man in the wheelchair. When Brendan got to him, he spent time with him, getting photos taken, signing his programme, asking about how he came to be a wheelchair user. The next night there was another wheelchair user in the queue and a member of the cast, who shall remain nameless, thought he'd use Brendan's line from the night before that had got everybody laughing. 'I see you brought your own seat,' he said, expecting the person in the wheelchair and the other fans standing in line to laugh. Instead, he got, 'Isn't that terrible, making fun of a person in a wheelchair?' and 'There's no need for that.' At this point, the rest of the cast were cracking up laughing at the cast member. But that was the thing: Brendan had a way of saying things that would get people laughing and that nobody would take offence at. It was like that with my mother. She hated bad language but had absolutely no problem when Brendan used it.

When I started working with Brendan back in 1991, a few months after I had been made redundant from EMI, I thought she wouldn't approve of my new job – and I was right. She thought I was taking a backward step in my career and she had a good rant about it.

'You're doing *what*? You were doing really well in EMI and you wouldn't even fight to keep your job. You were meeting the likes of Paul McCartney, Cliff Richard and Tina Turner and you gave all that up to go working for a comedian who works in pubs around Dublin. Are you mad? It's typical of you, though, always thinking of yourself. Don't mind me, who won't be able to sleep for worrying about you. You should go down to confession and tell the priest you broke your mother's heart.' And with that she took herself off to bed, slamming doors on the way.

'And don't come running to me when it all goes wrong,' she yelled from the landing, as her parting shot. SLAM went her bedroom door.

That went well, I thought.

You can understand my reluctance to invite her to a show!

At this time, I wasn't actually playing the role of Rory: Brendan and I were touring America promoting his book *The Mammy*. It had done really well in the States and we'd visited twenty-two cities in thirty days. We were bushed.

Then the actor who was playing Rory Brown at the time left to become a train driver. I kid you not. He was trying to get a mortgage and the banks wouldn't give him one because an actor's job wasn't seen as secure, so he'd jumped at the chance of a steady income. The only problem was that he had to leave quickly to be able to start his training.

New York was the last city of the tour, and Brendan only had to do one more reading. We were going to fly home to Dublin the next day, which was Sunday, and sail to Liverpool on the Monday to open a three-week sold-out run of *Mrs Brown's Boys* in the Royal Court, a 1,600-seat theatre.

I met Brendan for breakfast in Fitzpatrick's Hotel in Manhattan and he told me, in dramatic style, about the actor leaving to become a train driver. Then he added cheerfully, 'I don't have to worry, though, because you'll fill in. You're at the shows every night, so you know the lines.'

This was true, although I've always found learning my lines for the show quite difficult. I'd write down every line five times, just like doing lines in school – and God knows I'd had plenty of practice at that – then I'd cover them and read the lines before them to see if I could remember what came next. It would take me a whole weekend to learn the lines for one TV episode. For stage work, it's harder – there are a lot of lines and you have to get them immediately – you can't go back and re-record. The actor Simon Delaney gave me a great tip, which worked perfectly for me: 'Rory, the way to do it is, get the lines into your head and then record yourself speaking everyone's lines except your own – leave a gap on the tape. Then listen back to the recording and speak your lines into the space.' It worked like a charm.

Anyway, because Brendan was so cheerful, I thought he was joking about me playing the role and I went along with it. 'Ah, yeah, Brendan,' I said. 'I'll play the part, but I'll have to learn method acting so I can perform a camp character convincingly. I'm not sure I'd be able to play a gay man. Me going on stage? That's a good one … one of your funniest.'

'Rory, I'm serious. We go home tomorrow. I can't find an actor who's right for the part, who I can direct in a day and who can learn the lines in time. I'm sorry, but it has to be you.'

My face turned white. This wasn't a joke. 'Brendan,' I pleaded, 'I can't go on stage as Rory Brown. I've never been on a stage in my life.' This wasn't strictly true, but the Marist Brothers school plays didn't count. 'No! You'll have to come to some other arrangement.' At this point I was fanning my face with my hand in a mock-coquette manner, but the shock was real.

Brendan snorted laughing at my carry-on, but he didn't change his mind. 'Rory, you've got to do it. I can't get anyone else and if you don't do it, we'll have to pull the gig and there'll be no money to pay us during the summer.' That did it. I couldn't face not having any money for the summer. I'd just bought my first home and I had a mortgage to pay.

'Can I go out and buy my own costumes?' I asked.

'Yes.'

'Can I dye my hair blond?'

Brendan sat back. 'What do you want to do that for?'

'I want to be seen from the back of the theatre. Bruce Dickinson from Iron Maiden once told me that it's important to be seen all the way from the back of an arena.'

Brendan blinked, then threw his hands in the air and said, 'Yes, you can dye your hair if you want.'

'Right, then, I'll do it. But I've never acted before. If it all goes to shite, don't blame me,' I said, imitating my mother, except she would have said 'dust'.

'It'll be fine. I promise you. You're going to love being on stage,' Brendan reassured me. 'And just think: you can make Rory Brown the wildest, campest character ever. You just have to be yourself.'

Well, I couldn't argue with that, I suppose. So that's how I became an actor: a trained actor left the show to become a train driver and I filled in ... for almost twenty years.

But how to explain all this to my mother? Esther thought the only time you would be on telly or in the newspapers was if you were in trouble with the police. Normal, decent people never got their name in the paper. Now I had to phone her and tell her about my change in career – again – and that the following month I was going to be on *The Late Late Show*, performing a scene from *Mrs Brown's Last Wedding* alongside Brendan and Jenny Gibney, who plays Mrs Brown's daughter, Cathy.

I decided I'd call her from Liverpool, instead of telling her face to face. I reckoned that the best time to call her was Wednesday night at seven in the evening, half an hour before I was due on stage. That way, I'd have had my opening-night performance the previous night under my belt and I wouldn't feel as nervous. Also, I could end the call really quickly by saying I needed to get my costume and make-up on.

The immediate reaction when I phoned was one of suspicion. 'You were only up here the other day and now you're ringing me from Liverpool. What have you done?'

I wasn't going to play the game of talking around the houses but not getting to what I wanted to say. Instead, I decided to get it over with. I told her that I wasn't in any trouble and I hadn't got some girl into trouble either – wishful thinking on her part! I told her that I was still working with Brendan, but instead of booking the gigs and doing PR for him, I was getting a promotion and was joining him on stage as one of the cast. I thought that by dressing it all up as a promotion she might be more accepting. I was wrong.

'Dear sweet Jesus, I don't believe it,' she shrieked, her voice going up a few octaves. 'You won't believe this,' she said, holding the phone away from her to shout to Da: 'Our first-born has decided, at the age of forty, to become an actor. What do you think of that? Oh, my God,' she said, without waiting for my father to respond, 'that news might kill your poor father. You know he has a weak heart.'

So that's how quickly things moved with my mother: I tell her I'm going to be acting on stage and what she hears is that I'm trying to kill my father. Ah well, in for a penny in for a pound, I thought, and proceeded to tell her that, in less than a month, I was going to be on the biggest TV show in Ireland, playing the part of Mrs Brown's gay son Rory, with my hair bleached blond, doing a scene from a play.

'Hold it right there! Back up a bit. Tell me that again?' I repeated the bit about appearing on stage.

'Not that! Go back further.'

Trust her to home in on the part I wanted to gloss over. 'I'm playing the part of Mrs Brown's gay son, Rory, and my hair will be bleached and we're going to be on the telly performing a scene from the play,' I repeated, trying to be as cheery as I could. 'It's going to be fantastic promotion for the show we're doing in the Gaiety Theatre.'

There was a pause. 'Oh, Rory,' she sighed. 'Don't be going on the television being something you're not.'

I asked her what she was talking about.

'You know,' she said. 'Going on telly acting. People might think it's you being you and not realise you're only playing a part. Now, I've got to go. I've been promising myself a mud pack for the last week. You give up that aul acting. You don't want your name in the papers.' And with that, the phone went dead.

Brendan was helpless with laughter when I told him that Esther thought I was going on the telly playing the part of 'something I'm not'!

I hadn't come out to my parents, even though everybody knew I was gay. I had often thought of coming out to them but had always held back. Why rock the boat? The stigma attached to AIDS was still very prevalent, not to mention that homosexuality was still a crime and that discrimination against gay people ran right through Irish society. If I told my mother, I could imagine her saying afterwards to my father, when the two of them were at home alone: 'A man? Rory is looking for a man? Where did we go wrong? He was such a good boy. How did he turn into such a pervert? He must get that from your side of the family. There was never anything like that in mine.'

But when I did eventually tell her, after I'd appeared on the Miriam O'Callaghan show, the reaction was not like that at all. She was more than supportive. 'I just want you to be happy,' she said, 'and if you find a man that makes you happy, then you bring him home here to meet me. It's a pity you didn't tell me years ago. It would have saved me running around trying to fix you up with a girl. Now, don't say anything to your father. He won't understand.'

And that was true. My father was very religious, having found God after his heart attacks. He was also very innocent about anything outside of husband-and-wife relationships. It's not that he was anti-gay: he just thought all gay men in relationships were simply good friends.

So much wasted time, really, but that's what happens when you project thoughts and ideas onto somebody else. They never react as you imagine they will.

Years later, when my mother confided in her great friend Lily that I was gay, Lily asked if I could be cured. 'No, there's no cure,' Esther said.

Lily sympathised and said, 'Ah, God love him. And him doing so well in work.' Lily could understand a terminal illness more than she could understand an alternative lifestyle. And any time I met her after that, she'd look me over to see if I was showing signs of being terribly sick, shaking her head and saying, 'Ah, howya Rory?' in the same tone she'd use when saying, 'I'm sorry for your troubles' to a widow who'd just lost her husband. But as I said, many in the older generation had fixed ideas.

We finished the run in Liverpool in late June and we had the summer off. The three-week run had been so successful that all the cast and crew could be paid right through July and August, when we were off to allow Brendan to go home to his family. Brendan had come up with the idea of everybody, including him, being paid every week, instead of after a run, which was the usual practice. The budgets would be done for the beginning of each year and we got paid every week accordingly, even though we might not be working. It was a fantastic system. It inspired loyalty and, as we were all getting paid every week, we didn't have to go looking for work elsewhere, like many actors do, and the company didn't have to replace cast or crew who might have left to take up work somewhere else.

When September came along, we had three weeks booked in the Pavilion Theatre, Glasgow and then three weeks in the Gaiety Theatre, Dublin. I knew I'd have to bring Ma to one of the Dublin shows and I was dreading it. I thought, She'll hate me in the show and she'll be disgusted with some of the language. Then I remembered that she loved TV shows like *Steptoe and Son*, about a grumpy scrapyard worker and his hapless son, and *Till Death Us Do Part*, with the famous 'old git', Alf Garnett, as well as the *Carry On* films with their saucy double entendres. I reckoned that if she liked them she might possibly like our show.

I went home for my Sunday dinner as usual, and I asked if she and Da would like to come to see the show. 'Oh, I wouldn't miss it! My son on the stage of the Gaiety. I was talking to your Da about it and we think it'll be great to see you before you settle down and get a proper job.' I guess she never forgave me for not getting a job in a bank over twenty years before!

They decided they were going to go on the following Friday night. 'It'll give me time to get my good frock, and that blue coat you got me last year, cleaned. And I'll get my hair done on Friday instead of Saturday. I wonder if Mister Roche' – which she pronounced 'Rochay' – 'will mind if I change my appointment? Well, to hell with him if he does,' she declared, folding her arms across her chest. 'I'll just tell him that my son is on in the Gaiety and I need my hair done.'

Oh, God, I thought, what if she hates the show and the bad language? The next day I arranged good house seats for her and my father. I also made sure someone from the Gaiety front-of-house staff would make a fuss of them, get them drinks before the show and during the interval and generally make them feel special. When the show was over, they were to be brought back to the green room.

My mother was really impressed when I rang to tell her about the arrangements. 'I won't keep you. I must ring a few people,' she said, her voice full of merriment.

I was thrilled that all the shows were sold out, so they were going to see a full theatre howling with laughter, and on Friday night, the reaction from the audience was amazing. I was sure the laughs were the loudest of the week. The cheers, when the cast came out to take their bows, were huge. I dashed off to get my stage make-up and costume off so that I wouldn't be leaving Ma and Da waiting too long in the green room. And so that if they hadn't liked the show, I could get them out of the stage door before the rest of the cast arrived. But my concerns were misplaced. 'Rory, you were brilliant, and Mrs Brown was amazing. I don't think I've ever laughed so much in my life!' my mother gushed, a great big grin all over her face. 'And your da loved it, too, didn't you?' she said, nudging my father in the ribs.

'Rory, I can't tell you how great I thought that show was. It was just fantastic!' my father said, happier than I'd ever seen him.

'Can you introduce me to Brendan?' my mother asked excitedly. 'I just want to tell him how funny he is.'

Just then, Brendan walked into the green room. He knew my parents were in and he made a point of going up to them before he greeted any of the other backstage guests. 'Mrs Cowan, Mr Cowan, lovely to meet you both at last,' he said as he hugged both of them. Anyone who has met Brendan knows that he likes to hug.

'Oh, call me Esther,' my mother said in her posh voice. 'And he's Rory Senior, not Mr Cowan,' she gushed.

From that moment on, my mother wouldn't hear a word said against Brendan O'Carroll. 'He's a gentleman,' she'd say, rounding on anyone who had the nerve to complain about him or the bad language in the show. 'People use language like that all the time. It's used widely in all manner of conversation.' And when *Mrs Brown's Boys* became a huge hit on BBC and RTÉ, she was as proud as a peacock. 'My son is in *Mrs Brown's Boys*,' she'd boast. And if there were any further complaints, she'd cut them short. 'Does your television not have an off button, or a remote control to change the channels? Mine does.' And she'd be off, raising her voice just in case anyone beyond a twenty-yard radius couldn't hear her. 'Why on earth would somebody watch a TV show every week just to be offended?'

When the cast of *Mrs Brown's Boys* became well known, I started to get invites to lots of first-night openings and book launches and many other events. I decided to take my mother to one of these, a charity event in one of Dublin's five-star hotels. While we were in the bar waiting for the function room to open, this youngish woman, in her mid-thirties I would say, made her way towards us. I knew she recognised me and that she was coming over to talk to me. I also knew that she was everything Esther disliked in a woman. She had on too much make-up and jewellery, her face was puffy from long-term drinking and she was wearing a fur coat over a far-too-tight dress with red stilettos.

'It's you,' she drawled, pointing at me. 'You're the gay one from that awful television show, aren't you?'

Immediately, Esther jumped into action. 'Oh, thank you very much,' she said animatedly, her hands turned upwards in front of her. 'I was trying to remember that old Salvation Army recruiting slogan. Seeing you reminded me of it. It goes, "Thousands have come this way before, there's plenty of room for thousands more."' The floozy, as my mother would call her, flounced off, her face flushing a deep shade of crimson.

'Bravo,' said another woman, who'd overheard the exchange, to my mother. 'Are you always this vicious?'

'No,' Esther replied suspiciously, wondering if I was going to be insulted again: 'Sometimes I have laryngitis.'

'Oh, how fabulous. You're just too funny. You certainly put her in her place.'

'Well, she deserved it,' Esther responded. 'And as I always say, nobody is born with manners. We pick them up as we go along.'

When, in the early 2000s, things started to really pick up for the *Mrs Brown's Boys* group, Brendan began sending out hampers at Christmas. He'd send dozens to family and friends and people who had helped us, like Gay Byrne. My mother was included. She used to love getting these hampers every year. She'd have friends and relations in to forensically examine every item in the hamper. They'd take each thing out one at a time and then, after oohing and aahing over each one, they'd be put back in the exact same spot in the basket.

The first year Brendan sent a hamper, I happened to call up to see my mother a few minutes after it had been delivered. As it happened, my auntie Eileen was there for lunch. When I let myself in, I could hear my mother saying from the dining room, 'Ah, Brendan, he never forgets me. Eileen, he even includes me in his plays.'

Brendan had used her name in a scene where the characters Buster and Dermo are planning to break into a circus and rob jewellery, cash and fur coats. In the scene, Dermo asks Buster how they are going to fence the stolen goods. Buster replies: 'Jewellery, Donal Black; clothes, Esther Cowan; and any cash, we keep.' When she first heard her name mentioned on stage, my mother had yelped with delight, and when that scene was included in one of the TV episodes, she was overjoyed. People she hadn't heard from in years rang her up to say they had heard her mentioned on the telly. The parish priest congratulated her from the altar during ten o'clock Mass and the other Mass-goers gave her a round of applause. She was in her element.

But back to that first hamper. When I walked in through the front door, my mother called out, 'Rory, is that you?' as she came running out of the dining room. 'Quick,' she said in an urgent whisper, 'go into the front room and write down Brendan's phone number in my little address book. Now don't ask any questions, just do it.' And then, in her normal voice, she said, 'When you're ready, come in and say hello to your auntie Eileen.' With that, she went back into the dining room, saying, 'More tea, Eileen?'

I wrote the number down in my mother's little book beside the phone and went in to join her and my aunt. I knew she was up to something and I guessed it had to do with the phone number I had written out for her. 'Eileen,' she said, 'would you get that phone book over there and find Brendan O'Carroll's number for me? I don't know where I left my glasses and I won't be able to read the small writing.' And, as Eileen was looking for the number, my mother said, almost as if it was an afterthought, 'I really should have him on speed dial.'

I was impressed at how easily and convincingly my mother could lie. Granted, they were only little white lies, but she was a better actor than I was. Her performance was so good I nearly believed that Brendan was her best friend. As Eileen called out the number, my ma dialled it into her cordless phone and walked into the dining room, making sure Eileen could hear what she wanted her to hear. 'Hello, Brendan,' she said in her loudest posh voice. 'It's me, Esther.' Then, cupping her hand over the mouthpiece of the phone, she whispered so her sister couldn't hear her: 'Rory's mother.'

When Brendan had spoken to her, she raised her voice again and said, 'Thank you so much for the hamper, Brendan. It's beautiful. But you shouldn't be wasting your money on me,' breaking into peals of insincere merriment. Brendan replied, then my mother said, in the same jovial manner, 'You're a terrible man sending me such a magnificent hamper. I wasn't expecting anything from you, but I appreciate it very much. Very thoughtful of you. It's not like the usual old rubbish Rory gets me for Christmas.' As I gave her a stern look, she started the peals of laughter again. 'Bye-bye, Brendan. I'll talk to you soon.'

And with that, she hung up, looked at me as if she'd just noticed me and said, 'What are you doing standing there? Make yourself a sandwich and have it in here. Don't come into the front room. Eileen and I are talking and we want a bit of privacy.'

THIRTEEN

Everything I
Own

I am so glad that my parents got to see me in *Mrs Brown's Boys* and that they enjoyed every minute of it. Everyone thinks their parents will be around for ever, but the years slip by so quickly.

After Da had his two heart attacks in the 1980s he became a nervous man; the slightest noise would startle him. He also took early retirement from his job. He wanted to avoid all forms of stress. He got into breeding cats after visiting a cat show, where he bought two beautiful British Blues, with thick grey fur and orange eyes. He joined a cat club and his cats went on to win many awards at shows in Ireland and the UK. He made many friends in the cat world; he and my mother used to visit other cat lovers all over the country and they would visit my parents.

Breeding cats opened up a new social world for my parents and they did enjoy it. My father seemed happier and my mother, who was extremely outgoing anyway, was meeting new people. For the next fifteen years or so, they were very happy with their lives and were content growing old together. But life has a way of giving you a kick in the balls, and my father got just that kick in 2006, when his health started to take a turn for the worse. He found he couldn't walk as far as normal without getting out of breath and when he walked up the stairs, his breath was short when he reached the top. He always took the dog out for a walk, but now, a stroll that used to take him twenty minutes took an hour. He wasn't in pain, so he wasn't too bothered – he thought that, at seventy-five years, it was just old age catching up with him.

Eventually the shortness of breath became too much and his doctor recommended he go for tests. When the results came back a week later, he was told he had cancer in his lungs and a touch of it in his liver. A course of chemotherapy was advised and dates for the treatment set. The prognosis was good.

However, I think the day my father was told he had cancer was the day he started dying. He heard the word 'cancer' and all he heard was that he was going to die. I'm convinced of it. He visibly shrunk over the next few days. It was as if he'd decided his life was over.

My mother found great comfort in her faith. When we were children, she was adamant that we go to Mass every week. We also had to say decades of the rosary if we wanted something. For instance, when our Mini was stolen it was reported to the gardaí and they said they'd keep an eye out for it and do their best to get it returned as soon as possible, but this wasn't good enough for Esther – she wanted God's help. So every night, the family, except for my father, had to say a decade of the rosary to ask God to help get us our car back. We also said decades of the rosary if any family member was in hospital and needed God's help to get better.

The car was missing for over two weeks. It turned up, abandoned, in the city-centre area of Summerhill. A man who had a shop there noticed it had been parked in the same spot for days and became suspicious. This man got us our car back, but according to my mother, it was the nightly rosary that was the cause of our good fortune. When I asked why God had taken two weeks to hear us, I got a slap on the ear and was told, 'God is very busy.'

When my father was told he had cancer, the news floored him, even though the doctors told him that even if the chemo didn't work, because of his age, the cancer would spread very slowly. He didn't see this as being hopeful. He became frail and vulnerable almost overnight. My mother, who had recovered from breast cancer back in 1971, tried to encourage him to fight it, but he didn't seem to have any fight in him. He had problems with the chemo and asked his doctor to take him off it. I couldn't understand why he was giving in to the disease. I wanted to say, 'Da, give yourself a chance, fight this,' but I felt that might have upset him.

The family had a conversation with the doctors in the hospital and when the question was put to my father: 'Do you want to be resuscitated if your health deteriorates?' He replied, 'I want to live.' We pretended that this was a normal conversation and that it didn't mean anything, but my mother looked as if her world were falling apart. I think it was dawning on her that he might die. But she looked at my father and said, 'You're not dying on me now. If you were going to die, you should have done it years ago when I had a chance of finding another husband. I'm an aul wan now and haven't a hope of finding anyone else, so you're not dying on me and leaving me on my own.'

Even the doctor laughed, and for the first time since he was told he had cancer, Da laughed too. I knew the end was near, though. This conversation we had with the doctor wouldn't have happened if my father wasn't dying. I think my father and mother knew, too. Their fiftieth wedding anniversary was a couple of days later and at the family dinner to celebrate, my Da said he couldn't think of a better present than to have all his family around the table with him. My mother sat there patting his hand.

The following week Da was back in hospital for the final time. While he was there, he went into a coma. His brothers and sisters flew in from England and sat for days with Ma, Gerard, Maeve and me in the hospital. On the afternoon of 21 September 2008, my mother asked if she could have some time with him alone. His brothers and sisters left, saying they'd be back that evening. My mother asked me to go out for a cigarette. 'I want to talk to your father on my own,' she said, her voice cracking. I was a smoker then so I went down to the hospital car park for a ciggy. When I finished my second, I went back up to Da's room. I figured that my mother would have told him all she wanted to tell him by then.

When I got to the room, the only sound was Da's laboured breathing. My mother seemed more content than she'd been earlier.

'Well, did you say what you wanted to say?' I asked.

'I did,' she replied, 'and I feel much better now.' Suddenly, she looked at the bed and said in a very small voice, 'Rory, is he still breathing?' There was no sound coming from my father. I ran outside to get a nurse who came in, opened my father's eyes, shone a torch into them and just shook her head. 'I'm very sorry,' she said.

When I drove Ma home later that afternoon, the house was very quiet, unnaturally so. My mother sat down and just stared at the chair on the opposite side of the fireplace where my father used to sit. That was his chair, and for as long as I could remember, whatever chair was in that spot was his. If any of us kids were sitting in it when he came into the room, we'd just get up and sit somewhere else.

My mother stared at that chair, numb with shock, for ages. She didn't touch the cup of tea I made for her. Then the doorbell started to ring. Da's brothers and sister came and neighbours dropped in to offer their condolences. The house became very busy very quickly. And one thing I noticed was that my mother became a widow very quickly. That night, whenever she mentioned my father, she followed it up with, 'Lord rest him.' Until she got dementia a few years later, she always referred to him as 'My husband, Lord rest him.' I've spoken to many people about this strange phenomenon and they've told me that this is an Irish thing. It's a conversation shortcut. Once you say, 'My husband, Lord rest him,' it lets people know you are a widow and no more needs to be said on that subject.

And it's only a small part of the conversational shortcuts that Irish women have. The year after my father died, I took my mother to a Christmas variety show. A friend of mine, the fabulous actress Marion O'Dwyer, brought her mother, too. My mother and Marion's mother had never met before and after the introductions, I went to the bar to get us a drink. Marion joined me to help me carry the drinks back to the table. Now, we couldn't have been gone more than ten minutes, at most, but both women had learned everything they needed to know about each other's families. My mother told me that Mrs O'Dwyer was a widow. She told me how many children she had, what they did for a living, where they lived, what her husband used to work at, where she lived, how long she lived there and where she was originally from. In ten minutes. And when I spoke to Marion the following day, she told me that her mother had all the same information about my mother and her family. That's Irish mothers for you.

My father was, like so many Irish dads at that time, the head of the household. He needed to say very little for us to sit up and listen. But he was always there in the background and when it really mattered.

Looking back on it, Dad was the one who'd steadied the ship when, to my mother's disgust, I failed my Leaving Cert maths. He'd got me the summer job in EMI, because he understood me and knew what I really wanted. Nothing would have happened if Da hadn't got me that job. For the moments that changed my life, Da was always there in the background, supporting me, driving me into work, going in late at night if the burglar alarm sounded in the shop. When EMI was looking for redundancies when I was still working in the record shop, Dad worked out something for me and the other staff members in the shop, so that we had a package instead of the usual last-in-first-out routine. He looked after us.

Ma was the life force in the family, but Da was the one who made the decisions. He was strict and his mind couldn't be changed if he'd said no. He was a quiet person – but he'd argue about anything! That was his way, honed through years of talking politics. He taught me a lot about discrimination and workers' rights. He'd seen both sides of life, from having everything on Malahide Road, to living in Ballyfermot, and he passed it on to me. I hate snobbery and I don't buy into it – that comes from him. He and Ma made a great team.

My father's funeral was a hoot – unintentionally, of course. Even though we were heartbroken, my mother's antics brought a smile to our faces. Looking back, I think that this might have marked the early stages of my mother's dementia, because some of her reactions were, quite frankly, a bit odd.

I suspect that Ma had had dementia for quite a long time. About fifteen years ago, around 2004, she'd been taking the dog for a walk and fell – she had no memory of it, but it was a bad fall. A woman was driving by and saw Ma flat out on the pavement, the dog standing beside her, and she stopped and helped her up and Ma was very confused – she didn't know what had happened. So the woman put her in the car and got her home. We went to the doctor and of course Ma protested: 'I'm fine, I just had a turn.' We wondered if she'd had something like a mini stroke, but she was fine, in spite of the bruising all over her face.

But then other things started to go 'funny', such as her insistence on only using her medical card, which didn't quite make sense when she had health insurance. We suspected that something was kicking in but couldn't put our finger on it. I remember once there was a May procession, or something along those lines, in Dundrum, and the statue of the Holy Mary was to be paraded up the steep hill in Ballaly. Ma got very excited and put out her papal flags, the ones she'd had for the Pope's visit in 1979, for a local procession. Then she walked up to the priest to tell him that she'd be putting the kitchen table in the front garden, so he could say Mass there. He was very nice about it, but I suspected that something wasn't quite right.

When Da was first diagnosed with cancer, he'd say, 'Rory, she's driving me mad.' She'd forget things she'd said or done. Once, they'd gone into town and had spent the whole day there and they were both exhausted. Ma said to Da, 'Now, when you get home, go to bed and have a nice lie-in in the morning.' That will be brilliant, Da thought. The next morning, Ma came into the room at 7.30 a.m. and pulled the curtains back. 'Right,' she told Da, 'you're not to be hanging around in bed all day. You're not well and you need fresh air. Come on, we're going out.'

Now, my mother insisted that I take care of the funeral arrangements, which is normal for the eldest son, but when I booked one undertaker, she was adamant and made sure I change it, because the family always used another. What happened to her not wanting to be involved in making the funeral arrangements, I thought? And when I picked a coffin that I thought she'd like, I showed it to her and she said, 'No, that won't do. It's too dark. Your father wouldn't like that.'

'Ma, Da's not going to see the coffin, so there's nothing for him to like or dislike about it. Now why don't you just tell me what you want and I'll make sure you get it,' I said.

'No, I want you to organise everything,' she said forcefully, but everything I arranged she didn't like, or wanted changed. I think that her memory was fading even then, and she'd make a decision, then forget she'd made it.

'What about a priest'? I asked. 'Do you want the hospital chaplain to say a few prayers before Da goes to the Orthodox church?'

'I don't think so,' she replied. 'Your father wasn't a Catholic and the only Russian Orthodox priest available is doing the Mass in the church.' Needless to say, on the day of the funeral, when we were at the hospital to collect my father's body to bring him to the church, my mother was heard to say, 'It's a pity we don't have a real priest.'

A real priest. I had to stifle a smile. 'He didn't want one,' I reminded her. 'Remember, he wanted a Russian Orthodox one.'

'It's an awful shame,' she said. We can't even get a priest for him, what is the world coming to?' One day she didn't want one and the next day she did. Something wasn't quite right, but I put it down to the stress of the funeral.

When we got to the church in Harold's Cross, we had to wait outside while the coffin was brought in. It seems that an open coffin is the standard procedure in the Russian Orthodox Church. It is also the practice that everybody who is able has to stand. But my mother was completely bewildered. There we all were, standing around an open coffin, looking at my father's face, my mother constantly asking, 'Where are the seats?' Then the funeral service began. I quickly found out that in the Orthodox Church they sing the funeral, when an Orthodox priest came bounding out from behind a curtain and started singing. It was actually quite nice. Very different from a Catholic funeral, but very nice all the same.

'I don't know any of these hymns,' my mother blurted out. 'Would they not sing "Ave Maria" or something?' I was laughing so hard I had to pretend I was crying by covering my face with my hands and bowing my head.

'May God forgive you', she said to me, blessing herself quickly, 'for laughing in a church. This *is* a church, isn't it?'

She was also confused by the name Da was given. When my father changed his faith, he'd had to take another name in the Russian Church. He needed to have a saint's name, so he'd picked John. All the people in the Russian Orthodox community knew him as John, not Rory. And when the priest sang something along the lines of 'remembering the recently departed John', my mother looked at me and said, with more than a hint of despair, 'Who's John? My husband's name is Rory.' I felt terribly sorry for her.

Another Russian Orthodox tradition is that before they close it, mourners can put flowers in the coffin. My mother found it outrageous, observing at the top of her voice, 'You put flowers on the grave, not on the person.' Then someone went to put flowers on Da, and they still had the plastic wrapper on them. 'No plastic!' the priest said. They wanted the flowers to degrade naturally, but Ma loudly agreed. 'Exactly! Flowers on the grave, not in the coffin!'

Da had made great friends in the Russian Orthodox community and hundreds of people had turned up for the funeral, which Ma found confusing. There was one woman crying very loudly, a woman of Ma and Da's age, and it turned out that she'd known Da well. They'd often sit together and chat. 'What's *she* crying for? It's *my* husband that's dead. Don't tell me that your father had a fancy piece.'

'No, Ma,' I shushed her, eyeing Gerard and Maeve. 'She's just a friend.' Ma had always left this part of Da's life alone, so she didn't know anything about it.

I know funerals are sad events, but Ma's unintentional comedy performance had made us both happy and sad. Looking back, however, I can see that what some of us found amusing must have been very distressing for her, not fully understanding what was happening. I realise now that Ma's rejection of everything I'd tried to do with the funeral arrangements and her confusion in the church was not normal behaviour for her. At the time, I thought it was grief that was making her act the way she did, but now I'm not so sure. Maybe it was a mixture of grief and the early stages of dementia. I know she became helpless in some ways after my father died, particularly with the practical things. Da had done the everyday things, like paying bills, and when he died, she couldn't manage it. He had loved technology, and paid all his bills online, but Ma just couldn't understand it.

A few years before he died, I'd called over for dinner one Sunday and my father said to me, 'You won't believe what happened on Friday. Your mother was complaining I was on the computer too much. I told her I was talking to your auntie Sheila in Canada. I told her that Sheila could see when I was online and we could write messages to each other. Your mother couldn't understand how Sheila could know I was on the computer when she's in Canada and I'm at home in Dublin.'

I rolled my eyes to show I understood that my mother had fallen out with technology years before and the workings of computers were beyond her. It was just something she wasn't interested in.

'But this is the best bit,' my Da said, laughing. 'I told her I'd teach her how to use the computer so she could talk to her friends on it. I told her that Sheila even had a pen pal in India who she chatted to online every day.'

'And can this pen pal in India see when Sheila is on her computer in Canada?' my mother asked him. When my father told her she could, my mother started shouting: 'Switch that computer off. I don't want any aul wans from India, or anywhere else, looking into my house and knowing my business.' She thought that people who had their computers switched on at the same time could look into each other's houses and listen in to what people were talking about. They'd even be able to see them getting dressed or undressed. 'Dirty bastards,' she muttered. 'And you can keep that computer off.'

If my mother did have early-stage dementia when my father died, I'm happy he didn't live to see it. It would have broken his heart.

Ma's illness influenced my decision to leave *Mrs Brown's Boys* in 2017. Brendan was an incredibly generous employer and we all had our share of the profits from touring, merchandising and repeats of the TV show. Quite honestly, I felt as if I was winning the lottery every year. And when things got big and we were doing stadium tours, it was brilliant. We felt like rock stars, playing all the arenas, turning up with big articulated trucks with the stage gear inside. But what is it they say? Stardom is never the way you think it will be? There are compromises to be made, and it doesn't feel like fun any more. The journey towards the top with Mrs Brown was amazing, and for me, that was enough. Added to that, Ma was in Dublin, unwell and being cared for by Gerard and Maeve, while I was often on the other side of the world.

I'm sure that nobody wants to hear me complaining about my massive good fortune, and they'd be right. Life just could not get any better than those early years, touring the UK, then Canada, but I've always been a restless soul, and after a few years I wanted to try new things. I also wanted to be closer to Ma, because I knew that she wasn't well. And fame is a funny thing. It never really bothered me being photographed every time I was out somewhere – I quickly learned to be prepared for people to come up to me and ask me for an autograph or a selfie. People were generally lovely. The one line I used to get was, 'My mother/granny loves you.' My fans were women of a certain age, and that was fine by me!

I think if fame had come to me when I was younger, I'd have gone off my head, but we were all older at this stage, so we could handle it. It did amuse me, sometimes, seeing how other people reacted to me. Everyone wanted to be my friend and I often wanted to say, 'But it's only me. I'm still the same old Rory.' Thankfully, my friends kept me sane, the same pals I'd always had and who are still my friends. They stopped me getting above myself!

The other thing is, I always knew fame wouldn't last. Everything has a shelf life, unless you're Paul McCartney or Mick Jagger, Elton John or Rod Stewart. That kind of fame is rare, so I knew that, someday soon, it would somebody else's turn – that was the way it was. Fame is fleeting, and that's fine with me.

My lowest point was when I was on tour in Australia in 2016. I got word that my mother had days to live. I couldn't come home, because I could only take a week off for compassionate leave if my mother died – until then I was expected to fulfil my obligations to perform at every show we were booked to do. It was an insurance thing – I understood, but I still felt sick about it. I had to keep up a happy face, because that's what the fans would expect when I'd meet them at the stage door after the show, while inside, my heart was breaking. When the tour finished I was so worried on the plane home to Dublin, hoping and praying that Ma would pull through, and when she did, I realised that my priorities needed to change. I knew that if I wanted to be closer to my mother, I would have to leave *Mrs Brown's Boys*. Thankfully, I had a year to make up my mind before the next tour and in 2017, I handed in my notice and left in July. It was hard, after twenty-six years, but I have no regrets. I had the time of my life and wish Brendan and the gang all the best.

When my mother was in the early stages of dementia, not long after Da died, she could make me laugh. It was desperately sad to see her losing her mind, but if you didn't laugh at the situation, you'd cry. At the beginning of her illness she used to ask the same questions over and over again. Initially, I thought she was just being difficult, but when she began phoning me four or five times every morning, I knew something was wrong. 'What are my plans for today?' she'd ask uncertainly when I'd answer the phone.

'I'm taking you out to lunch and then I'm going to bring you back to my house for the afternoon,' I'd explain. Half an hour later, she'd ring again and ask me the same question. My brother Gerard, who was her main carer at this point, told me that she asked him the same question over and over again – but in the middle of the night. Ma would go into his room a number of times during the night, wake him up and ask what her plans were. When he told me this, it turned out that he hadn't had a full night's sleep in weeks. Even when I was on tour in Australia, Ma would call me to ask me to ring Maeve and get Maeve to ring her.

'Ma, I'm in Australia. You're in Dublin and Maeve's in Dublin. Why can't you just ring her yourself?' I'd say. You see, I didn't know what was wrong with her. I thought she was just being clingy and needy. Maybe I didn't want to face up to what was going on in her mind.

One day, after many phone calls, me assuring her in each of them that I was taking her to lunch, I knew something was really wrong. I'd driven over to collect her from Gerard to bring her into town. When I got there, I found that she was dressed in a suit and blouse that really looked well on her. She looked better than she had in months. The only thing she wasn't wearing were her shoes.

'You look great, Ma,' I said cheerfully. 'C'mon, put your shoes on and we'll go into town and have a nice lunch.'

My mother looked at Gerard. 'Where are my shoes?'

'They must be in your bedroom. Go up and put them on.' Off she went upstairs. Tramp-tramp, tramp-tramp, her slow steps sounded on the stairs, while we sat on the sofa waiting for her. A few minutes later, I could hear her coming down. I stood up, expecting that we'd be leaving immediately, and in walked my mother wearing nothing but her underwear.

'Ah, Ma,' my brother moaned. I'm ashamed to say that I burst out laughing. It was nervous laughter and it's something that I used to do a lot at the most inappropriate times. Needless to say, my mother wasn't impressed. 'You stop laughing at me,' she said, eyeing me up and down in a way that made me feel like a naughty boy. It was at that moment that I really knew that something was seriously wrong. I worried that she might be on her way to having a stroke, so Gerard and I agreed to make an appointment for her to see her doctor.

When we got to the doctor's surgery, she was gripped by fear. 'What am I going to tell this aul fella?' she asked, grabbing my arm. Now, this 'aul fella' was about twenty years younger than her and he had been her doctor for nearly thirty years.

'Just answer all his questions truthfully,' I replied.

'What seems to be the trouble, Esther?' the doctor said.

'Oh, nothing,' my mother said airily. 'I don't know why I'm here at all. There's nothing wrong with me.'

'How's the health?'

'Oh, it's wonderful,' she replied. 'Never felt better in my life.'

'And your memory?'

'Perfect,' Ma said confidently.

The doctor nodded, taking notes as he did so. 'And how do you sleep?'

'With my eyes closed.' It was a funny answer and I had to stifle the urge to laugh.

The doctor smiled. 'Do you know why you're here, Esther?'

My mother looked at him contemptuously and said, 'Because *he*', pointing to me, 'says I'm sick. Why do you think I'm here?' She looked at me and, rolling her eyes, said, 'Don't you pay him. He's a brutal doctor.'

I was pleased to see that I wasn't the only one amused by Ma: the doctor couldn't help smiling, but even so he said, 'I'll make an appointment for you to bring Esther for tests in the geriatric unit in St Vincent's hospital. They'll find out exactly what's wrong with your mother.'

I hate that term 'geriatric'. To me it implies that old people are clapped out and no use to society any more. I knew, though, that we had to go through with it to find out what exactly was wrong with our mother.

The day of the appointment at the geriatric unit, I collected my mother to bring her to the hospital. 'Why do I have to go there?' she asked, looking sternly at me. 'Waste of time,' she added, sniffing.

I tried to keep everything light and airy on the way. 'When we're finished in here, how about we go into town for lunch?' I said cheerily. She just sighed irritably. Her annoyance faded as we walked into the hospital, though, and she became more timid. She turned into a frail and vulnerable woman and her eyes were wide open in fear. 'You won't let them keep me in here, will you?' she asked in a small, anxious voice.

'Of course not,' I replied, turning away so I didn't have to see the fear in her face. 'We'll only be in here for a few minutes and then we'll go to lunch.'

I shouldn't have reminded her that I was going to bring her to lunch. 'Make it snappy,' she ordered the doctor. 'We've to go to lunch and we haven't all day to be hangin' around here.' She obviously wanted to take control of the situation.

The doctor promised her he wouldn't keep her long. They chatted away for a few minutes and she assured him she was in perfect health. 'There must be a mistake,' she said with the most surprising courtesy. 'I'm as fit as a flea.' The doctor took a few notes.

When she was asked about her memory, she said, 'I sometimes wish I didn't remember so much.'

The doctor nodded.

'I just have a few questions to ask, if you don't mind,' he said kindly.

'Work away,' my mother snapped.

'What's your name?' was his first question.

My mother looked at me with a scornful expression, as if to say, Is he serious? 'Esther,' she replied, rolling her eyes to heaven.

'Very good, Esther. And when is your birthday?'

My mother looked at me and shook her head and whispered, 'Stupid questions.' She then looked at the doctor and said acidly, 'Why, are you thinking of buying me a birthday present?' She's avoiding answering the question, I thought.

'It's the seventeenth of April,' the doctor said.

'Well done! But I know that,' she muttered, even though I knew she didn't.

'And what year were you born?' the doctor asked.

Esther stared at him blankly, then looked at me and then back at him and said nothing.

'It was 1933,' the doctor said.

'That's right!' Esther declared triumphantly. 'Well done.' She'd made it sound like he had given the correct answer to a question she had asked.

I just couldn't help it – I burst out laughing. 'I'm really sorry,' I said to the doctor apologetically. He smiled and dismissed my outburst with a small wave of his hand, obviously familiar with all kinds of reactions. It wasn't that I found my mother's memory issues amusing – quite the opposite. I was devastated.

The doctor asked her a number of other questions, which she either got wrong or didn't answer at all, such as who the president of Ireland was, what year it was, what day it was and so on. 'Now, Esther,' he continued, 'I'd like you to take this sheet of A4 paper in your right hand, fold it in half and then with your left hand, place it here beside the phone.' I couldn't believe my eyes when my mother took the sheet of paper in her left hand, crumpled it up and threw it over her left shoulder. Looking at me, she rolled her eyes and tut-tutted to herself.

The doctor asked me to step outside.

'Doctor, I'm really sorry about all that,' I blurted out. 'I don't find it funny, but none of what she told you in there is true,' I said anxiously.

'I know,' he replied. 'The tests I did and the questions I asked show that there is an issue, but as part of a wider assessment, I'd like your mother to have an MRI.' He told me she had been booked in for one when he got her GP's referral letter and if I was to take her down to the X-ray department now, they could do the scan.

It was only a short walk from the geriatric unit to the X-ray department. The radiologist who met us there was a young black man named James and he put my mother at ease immediately. He held her hand as he walked her into the room where the scan was to be done. He talked her through everything that was going to happen. He spoke to her in a soft, gentle voice and I could see she was charmed by him. My mother lay on the table and then the table was slid into a tube and a few minutes later, the scan was done. I thought she'd panic or wouldn't stay still, but she did. And I thought she might be claustrophobic, but she wasn't. The radiologist had made the whole experience so easy for her. I was impressed.

When we were leaving I asked when we could expect the results. James said they would go back to the professor in the geriatric unit and then he would forward them on to my mother's GP. 'They might want to see your mother again in about six months' time to repeat the tests and to have another scan,' he explained, 'just to see if there's any change.'

I looked at my mother and with forced jollity I said, 'You'll be coming back to see James again in a few months. You'll like that, won't you?'

She smiled at James and me and said, 'Oh, lovely.'

James went on to tell me that he wouldn't be here in six months' time. 'I'm moving to London in a couple of weeks,' he said. 'I'm getting a position there.'

Before I had a chance to congratulate him on his imminent move – BOOM! And of all the BOOM moments I encountered with my mother, this was the one that sent me reeling. 'You'll get a great job on the buses over there,' she said, patting James on the arm.

I gaped with shock. I couldn't believe what she had just said. Oh, God, just transport me to anywhere else this minute, I thought. My face was flushing a deep crimson.

'My husband worked on the buses in London years ago, before he was born,' she said, pointing at me. 'And fellas like you had great jobs on the buses with him. I'll ask him to put in a word for you,' she said, obviously forgetting her husband was dead. All I could do was stand there with my mouth wide open and stare at her in disbelief.

'She doesn't know what she's saying,' I stammered and then I stopped. James was laughing so hard his shoulders were shaking. Esther was blissfully unaware of what she had said and as I ushered her out as quickly as I could, she looked back and said to James, 'Look after yourself over there, son. And join a union.'

It's funny how things come around and the parent becomes the child. When I was a small child, I'd embarrassed her with my use of bad language and inappropriateness at the dental hospital near Trinity College. Now, as her dementia took hold, she became the one to embarrass me.

When I was five she took me to the dental hospital, beside Trinity College, to have a tooth taken out. The hospital was a training centre for dental students and it didn't charge patients, so that's why we'd ended up there. And because there was no charge, you could end up waiting for hours to be seen. After three hours, my name was finally called. At that time, they used gas as an anaesthetic and it had a very strange effect on me. Oh, it did the job and knocked me out, allowing a dental student, under the supervision of a qualified dentist, to extract the molar that was causing me pain, but as I was coming to, the anaesthetic made me say things I normally wouldn't, especially not in front of my mother. I told anyone within hearing distance that I knew curses, and to the amusement of everyone there, except my mother, I proceeded to reel off every swear word I knew, from fuck on. I stopped at nothing, saying every word I could think of, proud as punch. The dental nurses and the trainee dentists were howling and it must have encouraged me to tell them other swear words they might not be aware of, while my mother's mouth hung open with horror.

Esther bundled me up, saying, 'I don't know where he heard that language. He doesn't hear it in the house,' and she carried me off to catch a bus. 'You wait till I get you home,' was the last thing I heard before I fell asleep in her arms.

Now it was her turn to embarrass me. Oh, the irony of it. When my mother was mobile and could communicate, we used to go to the café in Marks & Spencer on Grafton Street two or three times a week. People with dementia do like routine and they like being where they are comfortable. They don't really like change, as I discovered. One time I took her to lunch in the five-star Westbury Hotel and afterwards I asked if she had enjoyed it. 'It was lovely,' she replied, 'but next time, can we go to the place we usually go to?'

The thing is, she loved the restaurant in M&S. The staff knew her and made a fuss of her and complemented her on her coat, even though it was the same coat she wore every day. Esther loved being made a fuss of. And even though the compliments were the same ones being repeated by the M&S staff every time I brought her there, they were always new to her when she heard them. She would be charmed. I'll never forget the wonderful M&S staff who were so kind to her.

Anyway, one day I took her for lunch in M&S again and while we were waiting to be seated the cleaner came over to say hello. She was a fan of *Mrs Brown's Boys* and always came over any time I was in the store. She had met my mother many times, too, and said, 'Hello, Mrs Cowan, you're looking well today.'

Out of nowhere, BOOM! Esther looked at her and, cocking her thumb in the cleaner's direction, said to me, at the top of her voice, 'I haven't a fucking clue who the hell she is. Tell her to fuck off.' The restaurant went silent and everyone looked over to see what was going on. I was mortified. Of all the people to use 'bad language', my mother was the last one you'd expect. She hated people swearing and this was the first time I had ever heard her curse. Thankfully, the cleaner saw the funny side too, 'She's having one of her days, is she?' she asked. I could only apologise and explain that my mother didn't know what she was saying.

This was one of the funny moments in my mother's last years, but dementia is a terrible illness, robbing sufferers and their families of happiness. It affected her in countless practical ways. My ma was one of those people who, if she changed a sofa at home, she'd have to have a new carpet and new curtains too, but when Da died, she had no interest in anything. She would clean the house, but the idea of doing it up was too much for her, because it was something they'd always done together. Da would go along with Ma, and they'd pick what she wanted, but he'd give the nod, 'Oh, yes, Esther, you've got great taste,' even though he couldn't care less. If there was a choice of two options, Ma would say, 'What do you think, Rory, which one will we get?' and he'd reply, 'Which one do you like?' Anything for an easy life.

Everything at home started to get old and faded after Da died – you could nearly see the floor underneath the carpets and the curtains were worn. I was in *Mrs Brown's Boys* at this stage and I thought, I'll get the whole house done up. We need new curtains and carpet, a new sofa and chairs.

But then the HSE nurse came in to see Ma. I was embarrassed: she knew that I was in *Mrs Brown's Boys* and I worried that she'd think that I was keeping my mother in a state because I was too mean to spend money on the place. So I told her about my plans and she said, 'No, don't you dare do that, Rory. Your mother knows where she is at the moment. If you change it, she'll think she's in a home and she won't settle, and she'll get very agitated and want to go "home".'

I could see what she meant, so we didn't change anything. No wallpaper or new curtains – one curtain was even hanging off the rail and I couldn't do anything with it. It reminded me of Miss Havisham in *Great Expectations*, but I could also see how important it was to my mother, and it helped her to live at home for as long as possible. All we could do was clean and hoover. When I'd visit, I used to take down one of her collection of Toby jugs. 'Do you remember this from Ballyfermot?' I'd ask.

'Ah, yes,' she'd say, but I suspected that this was just to be agreeable. She didn't understand what I was talking about. Sometimes, though, she'd reach out and take them and examine them and I knew that she still had that connection to things. The HSE nurse had been absolutely right and knowing this really helped.

In the end, Ma's death came quickly. Because she'd been declining for over four years, I had assumed she'd just go on like this for ever – even though I dreaded it at the same time, because her quality of life was so diminished.

One day, the doctor came up and I said, 'She's not looking great, is she?'

'Well, she's no spring chicken,' he replied, unnecessarily.

'Well, she's got as many chemicals in her as one,' I shot back. Poor Ma was a huge amount of medication at the time, to manage pain and anxiety as well as a whole host of other symptoms.

The doctor had always warned us against Ma becoming dehydrated, and told us that, if she refused to take water, we should ring the hospital, quick. One evening Maeve, who'd been visiting our mother, rang me and said, 'I can't get Ma to drink. I'm going to ring for an ambulance.' Ma was swiftly taken into A&E in St Vincent's Hospital. Then Maeve called me to say that Ma was on a drip and was doing okay.

I was recording the *Podge and Rodge* show in RTÉ in Donnybrook and I popped in to see Ma afterwards. She was in a cubicle in a very crowded A&E and initially I thought, God, she's eighty-five years of age, but then I realised that she was getting her fluids, so she was doing fine. Gerard and Maeve went off for a much-needed break when I got there and I sat down beside Ma, who was fast asleep. The next thing, a number of alarms went off and with that, a lot of medical people came in and started switching them off and doing tests.

One of them, a woman, said, 'Your mother is dying now. She's not going to last. Do you want resuscitation?' It was amazingly blunt, but then, there was no time to waste.

With a heavy heart, I said no.

Another medic said, 'Ring your brother and sister and tell them to get here now. We'll bring her into the imminent death suite.' This might sound macabre, but in reality it was a lovely place, quiet and calm. The doctors were right. Ma only lasted another hour, and we were all gathered around her when her breathing finally stopped.

It was bittersweet – I was happy and sad at the same time. Happy because she immediately looked more peaceful, her face relaxed. Sad because she was gone. She died on Monday morning, 5 November 2018.

Maeve, Gerard and I had to organise Ma's funeral then, which provided light relief, in its own way, with the three of us arguing about everything. Ma liked mahogany, so we picked a mahogany coffin, but then Maeve said she wouldn't like that. That's the thing about death, I find, happiness and sadness mingle. I was sad that Ma couldn't be laid out at home because the house was in a very threadbare state, but the funeral home did an excellent job.

My assistant Avri was fantastic, even if he did amuse me once or twice. When he came to the funeral home, he stood at my mother's coffin for a good twenty minutes, just looking at her. He's praying, I thought fondly, but then he turned to me and said, 'I've never seen a dead body before!' He was the most amazing help to me and he took so much weight off us. He was a rock. When we came out of the church, all the old people from the old folks' club that she'd attended every week made a guard of honour for her. Even until the end of her life, her carer would appear every week and take her up to the club. Poor Ma didn't know what was going on, but everyone would say hello and offer her cups of tea and talk to her, even though she had no awareness.

For all of us, losing our mother was terribly hard. We were relieved that her suffering was at an end, but she was our mother; and who ever wants their parents to die? It's part of life, but that doesn't make it any easier.

Since Ma's death, I know that Gerard has found life easier, because he did so much of her care during her last years, but we miss her, her fiery wit and her bravado. Without Ma, I don't think I'd ever have set foot on stage or believed in myself enough to do all that I've done in life. She was the centre of our world: sometimes fierce, often hilarious, but she meant everything to us.

Rest in peace, Ma.

EPILOGUE

True Colours

These days, the question I get asked most, especially since *Mrs Brown's Boys* started on BBC One, is, 'Are you in a relationship?' Most people are surprised when I say I'm not. 'I don't know how a lovely fella like you hasn't been snapped up,' is the usual response and while I'm flattered, the fact is, I'm not in a relationship and I don't expect to be in one in the future. I'm sixty and I'm too set in my ways. Relationships are compromises and I don't really compromise. And I've always been that way. I go where I like, do what I like when I get there, eat what food I like, watch what I like on TV, stay in if I like or go out if I like. I don't need to think about what another person in my life wants to do and I don't have to compromise or make concessions for their preferences. It might sound selfish, but that's the way it is for me.

Another reason that I'm not in a relationship is because I think my time has passed. Back in the late seventies or the eighties, I could and should have been in a few long-term relationships before I found Mr Right, but it was too difficult to maintain a gay relationship in those days. How would they have worked when gay relationships were dismissed as not normal, or written off as unnatural? Most gay relationships, for the while they lasted, were mostly kept secret from family and work colleagues, which wasn't easy. Unlike straight couples, when there was trouble in the relationship or marriage, gay couples didn't have family and friends for support, advising them on how to work things out. And while many straight couples stayed together for the sake of the children, that was not the case back then for people in same-sex relationships. So there was no expectation, even by many gay people, that gay relationships would last.

Back then, there were so many reasons for people to try to make straight relationships work. You stayed together for the children. You stayed together because you couldn't afford to run two homes. You stayed together because it was just too difficult to look at everything you owned together and divide it up. It was actually quite difficult to break up a straight relationship back then. Gay people who split up in the seventies and eighties just had to take their toothbrush and move out. Their families and workmates probably didn't even know about the relationship anyway, so they couldn't offer advice or try to convince them to stay together.

So that's the background I came from at a time when I could have been looking for a relationship. But apart from that, there was also the fact that I, and many other gay people in Ireland at that time, didn't know how to function in a relationship. We had all been brought up to be straight boys and girls. The assumption was that we were going to grow up, get a job, meet someone of the opposite sex, get married and have children. These were the values we were taught and this was the accepted attitude of that time. And the morals that were drummed into us were based on those assumptions. So, when in our teens or early twenties, we realised we were gay, we saw that everything we'd been brought up to believe just didn't fit into the way we were. We were taught that gay sex was unnatural and immoral. Gay people were seen as perverts. There were laws against us, for God's sake. Not only was the wider world not supportive of gay relationships, but gay people themselves weren't up to speed on how to function in a relationship. We had a group of young gay men and women who had no framework for their gay lives, so how could gay relationships work?

I could have regrets, but I know that I've been very lucky in life. I've been able to do what I want to do, to live life on my terms, and the future looks good. I hope still to be acting – watch this space! – and to work on a few new projects. I'm not ready to hang up my boots just yet! Thankfully, what I have now is the judgement and wisdom that I didn't possess all those years ago, when I was gallivanting around the place with Justin. I never worried about anything at that age, but the difference between the young teenage me and the me of today is that these days, I always try to think what the consequences of my actions might be. That's all part of growing up, I suppose.

In 2017 *The Big Issue* magazine asked me to write a letter to my younger self, offering words of wisdom. It was a great opportunity to look back over my life and to get it into some perspective. Here's what I wrote to my seventeen-year-old self.

Dear Me,

You've started a new job you love, in a record shop owned by EMI, in O'Connell St, Dublin. You're earning £21.50 per week and you're getting paid to do something you'd do for nothing at home; play records all day long. It's the perfect job for you and probably the most enjoyable job you'll ever have. You're off to a great start to your working life.

In school, you showed a talent for maths and your mother decided 'a job in the bank' would be the ideal job for you. 'It's a job for life, with a good pension and favourable mortgage rates for employees,' she insisted. You couldn't think of a job you'd like less, so you deliberately failed maths in your Leaving Cert, to make sure your mother couldn't nag you into taking a job in a bank. Instead, you got a job that you loved, in a record shop, to your mother's horror.

Contrary to popular belief, and certainly to your mother's, your job in a record shop won't be a dead-end job. In seven years, you'll end up being the sales and marketing manager of EMI Ireland, and you'll work with people like David Bowie, Queen, Paul McCartney, Kate Bush, Diana Ross, The Pet Shop Boys etc. Don't worry about how your mother sees your job. In 1988, you'll take her out to dinner with Cliff Richard and she'll accept that you're doing well.

Follow your own path in everything you do. If anyone gives you career advice, just don't listen. Don't listen to anyone who says, 'You must find something practical to do,' or 'You must have a real skill to fall back on, or a pensionable job.' Never look at a job doing something conventional or sensible, because you'll only end up doing work that doesn't make you happy. Deep down, you know what's best for you.

Stop trying to have girlfriends. They'll only end up being friends anyway, because you know, in your heart of hearts, that you have no sexual interest in girls and you never will. Save yourself six more years of hiding in the closet. In seventies Dublin, gay people are 'queers', 'poofs', 'bent', etc., and you are doing everything in your power not to think of yourself as gay, because being gay is different – and not in a good way, you think, in 1977.

I know you're putting the 'gay thing' to the back of your mind, afraid of being found out, afraid that if your friends discover your secret, they'll turn against you and you'll have no friends left, but the opposite is true. When you come out, in six years' time, not one single friend of yours will abandon you. They won't care one bit. In fact, they'll be delighted to have a gay friend and they'll think that your coming out is great news. You'll meet some fantastic friends on the gay scene, too, like Ken and Robert, who will still be your best friends in forty years' time. You're a teenager and you want to be part of a group. There's one waiting for you if you just pluck up the courage and go to them. Don't waste your time trying to hide who you are.

Last, but not least – stop trying to please everyone. It's impossible to do. Learn how to please yourself and don't deliberately do any harm to anybody. That way, you'll get to your late fifties with no regrets whatsoever, and you'll be able to look back and say, 'I've had a terrific life.'

Hey, by only working at jobs you love you'll even end up being famous – hahahahaha! You're going to have a fantastic life with much to celebrate, especially in 1993 and 2015, and when the losses come, as they inevitably will, you will be ready for them. Losing your mother and father will be the toughest thing you'll ever face, but you will face it, and you'll keep going. After all, there's nothing else to do, is there? That's all any of us can do.

Lots of love,

Rory Cowan

ACKNOWLEDGEMENTS

With huge thanks and lots of love to Ali and Audrey; Claudia Carroll; Marianne Gunn O'Connor; Pat Lynch; Sarah Liddy; Ken Hutton; Robert Doggett; Annette Carroll; Seán Dawson; Cian, Eoin, Oran and Evan Hillary; my sister Maebh and my brother Gerard; Avri Citron; Derek Mooney; Alan and Karl.

And to absent friends, of which there are many, who I'll never forget.